D1276579

AMERICAN
WAR MEDALS
and
DECORATIONS

AMERICAN WAR MEDALS and DECORATIONS

Newly Revised and Expanded

by Evans E. Kerrigan

A Studio Book

THE VIKING PRESS

New York

Original edition published in 1964
Revised edition issued in 1971 by The Viking Press, Inc.
625 Madison Avenue, New York, N.Y. 10022

Published simultaneously in Canada by
The Macmillan Company of Canada Limited

SBN 670-12101-0
Library of Congress catalog card number: 77-124322

Printed in U.S.A.

To my wife

CONTENTS

Part One: Decorations

Part Two: Service Medals

Part Three: Awards to Civilians

Supplement, 1970

ACKNOWLEDGMENTS

This book would have been impossible without the assistance I have received. Foremost I must mention my wonderful wife, Betty Ann, who encouraged me by her work and assistance. Thanks to my sister, Mrs. Elizabeth Fassig, for her many hours of labor editing the material, and to Mrs. Evelyn Werdelin, who did the typing.

My thanks also to Major R. F. Prentiss and Lieutenant S. H. Young, U.S. Army; M. C. Griffin, Head of the Decorations and Medals Branch, U.S. Navy; V. P. White, Head of the Decorations and Medals Branch, U.S.M.C.; Colonel James E. Mills, Colonel Cliff Atkinson, Jr., and Lieutenant Colonel John H. Magruder III, all of the United States Marine Corps; and to Major Gene Guerny and Captain Joseph A. Skiera of the United States Air Force Office of Information. Sincere appreciation is given to Captains R. L. Mellen and W. K. Thompson, Jr., of the United States Coast Guard, Public Information Division; R. A. Chandler, of the Maritime Administration, U.S. Department of Commerce; Colonel Gareth N. Branerd of the Selective Service System; and Mr. Patrick A. Gavin of the National Aeronautics and Space Administration.

Special thanks also to the National Geographic Society; to Jane Blakeney, former Head of the Decorations and Medals Branch, U.S. Marine Corps.; to some of my fellow members of the Orders and Medals Society of America; and to Norm Flayderman of Greenwich, Connecticut, for lending the Medals of Honor and other medals from his private collection for the purpose of photographing them.

To the many people who permitted me to borrow generously from their private experiences and to those who granted permission for stories of members of their families to be used in this book, I am grateful.

Thanks also to John C. Latham and Alfred J. Abbott and the many others who allowed me the use of their personal experiences.

—E. E. K.

INTRODUCTORY NOTE

"The road to glory in a patriot army and a free country is opened to all," General George Washington wrote when he established our country's first award for soldiers. The Badge of Military Merit, which he created in an order to the Continental Army on August 7, 1782, was probably the first official award ever given to officers and enlisted men without regard to their rank. Although this democratic decoration, a piece of cloth in the form of a heart, was a general one commemorating acts of unusual gallantry, it was the forerunner of our present Purple Heart, which honors those who have been wounded in action.

The Badge of Military Merit went out of use after the Revolution, and the nation was without an official decoration until the Medal of Honor was created during the Civil War. In 1905, Congress established the Certificate of Merit Medal, and in 1918 it authorized several more decorations to commemorate achievements in World War I: the Distinguished Service Cross, the Navy Cross, the Distinguished Service Medals, and the Silver Citation Star. Thus originated our "Pyramid of Honor," the system of individual decorations that has the Medal of Honor at the top, and following it, in order of precedence, the Distinguished Service Cross, Navy Cross, Air Force Cross, Distinguished Service Medals, Silver Star Medal, Legion of Merit, Distinguished Flying Cross, Soldier's Medal, Navy and Marine Corps Medal, Coast Guard Medal, Bronze Star Medal, Air Medal, Commendation Medals, and Purple Heart.

A military decoration—always in a distinctive shape such as a cross, a star, or a hexagon—is conferred on an individual for a designated achievement, whether combat or noncombat; the service medals—they can be distinguished from decorations because they are circular—are for all those who have served in a particular campaign, expedition, occupation duty, or emergency service. Ribbon bars, which are worn in place of the decorations and medals on all but a few exceptional occasions, are of the same material and design as those of the suspension ribbon awarded with the medal; each is a regulation ⅜ inch wide and equal in length to the full width of the suspension ribbon. Some ribbon bars denote awards that have no medal, such as the Presidential Unit Citation or the Navy Unit Commendation.

Small auxiliary insignia are also authorized to be worn on the ribbon or ribbon bar; a gold star, for example, signifies a subsequent award of a Naval Service decoration or medal. A bronze star worn on a Presidential Unit Citation ribbon indicates that the wearer has participated in the action for which the unit is honored; when it is worn on a campaign ribbon, a bronze star indicates participation in a specific battle, and a silver star equals five bronze stars. A bronze oak-leaf cluster indicates a subsequent award of certain Army and Air Force medals; a silver cluster indicates five identical awards. A small bronze "V" is worn on the ribbon of the Legion of Merit, the Bronze Star Medal, or the Commendation Medals to indicate participation in combat. Other such devices are mentioned in the descriptions of medals in the text.

Decorations and other official awards are authorized in several ways, most frequently by Congress, the President, or the Secretary of the Army, Navy, or Treasury. (Some commemorative and early semiofficial medals have been initiated by Army Department commanders.) Medals have been designed by famous artists; James Earle Fraser, Francis D. Millet, and Paul Manship are a few of the names that occur in this book. Others are the creations of the United States Mint, the Heraldic Section of the Army Quartermaster Corps, or a similar organization. Each is intended to be a distinctive symbol of a nation's gratitude to its citizens.

COLOR PLATES

Color Plate I

1. Army Medal of Honor, 1862-1896
2. Army Medal of Honor, 1896-1904
3. Army Medal of Honor, 1904-1944
4. Army Medal of Honor, present style

5. Navy Medal of Honor, 1862-1913
6. Navy Medal of Honor, 1913-1919
7. Navy Medal of Honor, 1919-1942
8. Navy Medal of Honor, present style

Color Plate II *Overleaf*

1. Medal of Honor
2. Brevet Medal, Marine Corps
3. Distinguished Service Cross
4. Certificate of Merit
5. Navy Cross
6. Soldier's Medal
7. Navy and Marine Corps Medal
8. Coast Guard Medal
9. Bronze Star Medal
10. Air Medal
11. Specially Meritorious Medal
12. Distinguished Unit Citation
13. Presidential Unit Citation
14. Navy Unit Commendation
15. Air Force Outstanding Unit Award
16. Good Conduct Medal, Coast Guard
17. Organized Marine Corps Reserve Medal
18. Naval Reserve Medal
19. Dewey Medal
20. Sampson Medal
21. Civil War Campaign Medal
22. Indian Campaign Medal
23. Expeditionary Medal, Marine Corps
24. Expeditionary Medal, Navy
25. Spanish Campaign Medal
26. China Campaign Medal
27. Cuban Pacification Medal

28. Nicaraguan Campaign Medal, 1912
29. Mexican Service Medal
30. Haitian Campaign Medal, 1915, 1919-1920
31. Yangtze Service Medal
32. China Service Medal
33. American Defense Service Medal
34. American Campaign Medal
35. European–African–Middle Eastern Campaign Medal
36. National Defense Service Medal
37. Korean Service Medal
38. Armed Forces Reserve Medal
39. Marine Corps Reserve Ribbon
40. Air Force Longevity Service Award
41. Merchant Marine Combat Bar
42. Merchant Marine Defense Bar
43. Merchant Marine Atlantic War Zone Bar
44. Merchant Marine Mediterranean–Middle East War Zone Bar
45. Merchant Marine Pacific War Zone Bar
46. Distinguished Civilian Service Medal
47. Outstanding Civilian Service Award
48. Exceptional Civilian Service Medal
49. Meritorious Civilian Service Award
50. Distinguished Public Service Award, Navy

1

2

3

4

5

6

7

8

Plate I

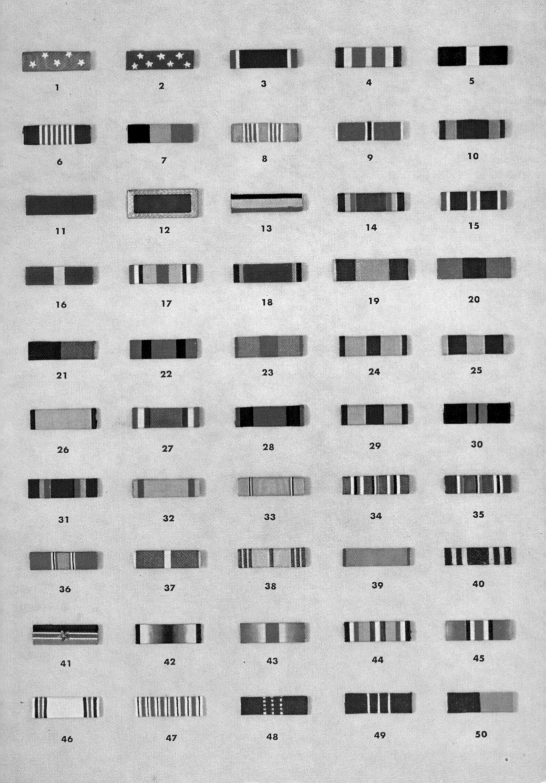

1 2 3 4 5

6 7 8 9 10

11 12 13 14 15

16 17 18 19 20

21 22 23 24 25

26 27 28 29 30

31 32 33 34 35

36 37 38 39 40

41 42 43 44 45

46 47 48 49 50

Plate II

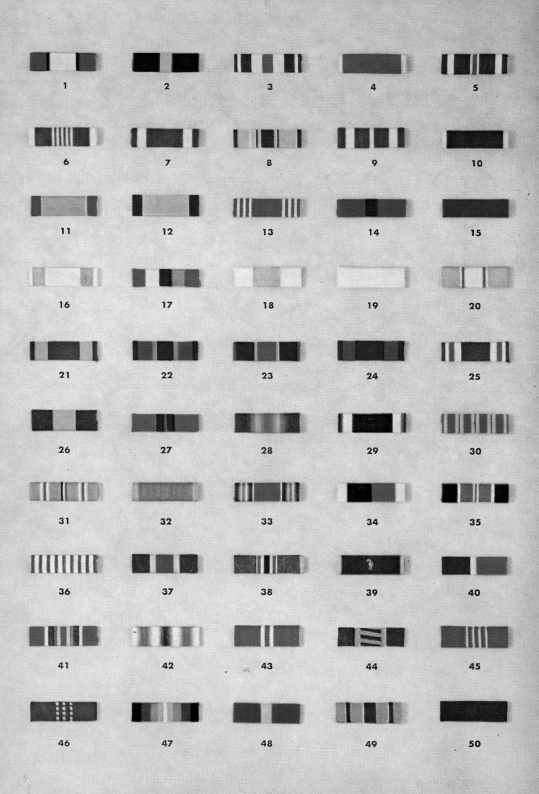

Plate III

Plate IV

Color Plate III

1. Distinguished Service Medal, Army
2. Distinguished Service Medal, Navy
3. Silver Star Medal
4. Legion of Merit
5. Distinguished Flying Cross
6. Commendation Medal, Army
7. Commendation Medal, Navy
8. Commendation Medal, Air Force
9. Commendation Medal, Coast Guard
10. Purple Heart Medal
11. Gold Life Saving Medal
12. Silver Life Saving Medal
13. Good Conduct Medal, Army
14. Good Conduct Medal, Marine Corps
15. Good Conduct Medal, Navy
16. Peary Polar Expedition Medal
17. NC–4 Medal
18. Byrd Antarctic Expedition Medal
19. Second Byrd Antarctic Expedition Medal
20. United States Antarctic Expedition Medal
21. Spanish War Service Medal
22. Army of Cuban Occupation Medal
23. Army of Puerto Rican Occupation Medal
24. Philippine Campaign Medal
25. Philippine Congressional Medal
26. Mexican Border Service Medal
27. Dominican Campaign Medal
28. Victory Medal, World War I
29. Occupation of Germany Medal
30. Second Nicaraguan Campaign Medal
31. Asiatic Pacific Campaign Medal
32. Women's Army Corps Service Medal
33. Victory Medal, World War II
34. Occupation Service Medal
35. Medal for Humane Action
36. United Nations Service Medal
37. Merchant Marine Distinguished Service Medal
38. Merchant Marine Meritorious Service Medal
39. Merchant Marine Gallant Service Citation Bar
40. Mariner's Medal
41. Merchant Marine Victory Medal, World War II
42. Merchant Marine Korean Service Bar
43. Medal for Merit
44. National Security Medal
45. Medal of Freedom
46. Air Force Exceptional Service Award
47. Distinguished Service Medal of NASA
48. American Typhus Commission Medal
49. Selective Service Medal
50. Bailey Medal

Color Plate IV

1. Brevet Medal, Marine Corps
2. Navy Cross
3. Distinguished Service Cross, Army
4. Distinguished Service Medal, Navy
5. Distinguished Service Medal, Army
6. Silver Star Medal
7. Legion of Merit (Officer)
8. Distinguished Flying Cross
9. Navy and Marine Corps Medal
10. Soldier's Medal
11. Bronze Star Medal
12. Air Medal
13. Commendation Medal, Navy
14. Commendation Medal, Army
15. Purple Heart Medal
16. Distinguished Service Medal, Merchant Marine
17. Meritorious Service Medal, Merchant Marine
18. Mariner's Medal, Merchant Marine
19. Meritorious Service Medal, Navy and Marine Corps
20. Certificate of Merit Medal, Army

PART ONE
DECORATIONS

MEDAL OF HONOR

Army

The Medal of Honor, instituted during the Civil War as a decoration to be conferred in the name of the Congress on members of the United States armed forces, is our nation's highest award for valor. It is granted to any person who, while an officer or an enlisted man in the Army of the United States, shall have distinguished himself by gallantry and intrepidity at the risk of his life, above and beyond the call of duty, in action involving actual combat with the enemy. Unlike the corresponding decoration for the Navy, the Army Medal of Honor has not, except under special circumstances, been awarded for action other than combat.

1862–1896

The first Medal of Honor, authorized by Congress on July 12, 1862, was the same as the Navy Medal, authorized a few months earlier (see page 8), with a different suspension. The medal itself, designed by Christian Schussel and engraved by Anthony C. Paquet, is a bronze five-pointed star. In the arm of each trefoil-tipped point are sprays of laurel and oak. The medallion in the center is rimmed by thirty-four stars, representing the states of the Union before Secession, and shows the goddess Minerva, symbolizing America, repulsing with the shield of the United States the crouching male figure of Discord. The reverse of the medal is blank; the recipient's name, rank, and unit, and the date and place of the action for which the Medal of Honor was awarded were customarily engraved in this space.

The medal is suspended from a clasp showing an eagle, wings spread, perched on two crossed cannon above a stack of eight cannon balls. The suspension ribbon is a variation on the American flag, with a plain blue field above thirteen vertical stripes of red and white. The bar pin above bears the shield of the United States, with a laurel branch and a cornucopia on either side.

1896–1904

Though the medal itself, the suspension bar, and the clasp remained the same, the ribbon on the 1862 Medal of Honor was changed by War Department orders dated November 10, 1896, to a white center stripe flanked on either side by a wide blue stripe, these in turn flanked by red (see color plate I, no. 2).

On February 14, 1898, it was announced that the suspension bar, ribbon, and medal would be affixed to a broad neck ribbon of the same three colors. However, the Medal of Honor continued for sometime to be worn as a breast decoration.

1904–present

Because the original Medal of Honor had been copied by certain veterans' organizations, the decoration was redesigned in 1904 by Major General George L. Gillespie, U.S.A., and the patent on his design transferred to the Secretary of War, so that further imitations of the award could be prohibited by law.

The present medal is a gold-finished star, its five points tipped by trefoils, superimposed on a laurel wreath of green enamel. In each point of the star is a green enamel oak leaf. The medallion in the center bears the head of the goddess Minerva, emblem of righteous war and wisdom, encircled by the words "United States of America." On the reverse, above the space for the recipient's name, is the inscription "The Congress to."

The medal is suspended from a horizontal bar bearing the word "Valor," with above it an American eagle, wings spread, grasping laurel leaves in one claw and arrows in the other. The eagle is fastened by a hook to a ribbon or pad of light blue, studded with thirteen white stars.

Though this new form of the Medal of Honor was originally intended as a breast decoration (see color plate I, no. 3), it could be worn around the neck. Also, since 1944 it has been given with a neck cravat of light blue, which has a star-studded light blue pad of octagonal shape in the center.

In 1916, as a further measure to protect this highest decoration, a board was created to investigate the 2625 Medals of

Honor that had been awarded to members of the Army up to that time. On February 15, 1917, 911 names were stricken from the list, and those in military service at the time were directed to return their Medals to the War Department for cancellation. Among those from whom the honor was withdrawn were 864 members of the 27th Maine Regiment, which had been awarded the Medal of Honor as a unit for its defense of Washington in June 1863. In fact most of the regiment had seen no action at that time; only about three hundred of its officers and men had stayed on to defend the capital, while the rest went home to Maine to be mustered out. Also removed from the list was the name of Dr. Mary T. Walker, of the Army Medical Corps, the only woman ever to be awarded the Medal of Honor. She had been cited by President Lincoln for her brave work in saving lives during the battle of Gettysburg, July 1-3, 1863.

Very few Medals of Honor were awarded during the actual fighting of World War I; only four were approved between April 6, 1917, and the Armistice on November 11, 1918. General John J. Pershing, however, was a firm believer in recognizing merit in the enlisted men as well as the officers under his command. He urged his unit commanders to submit recommendations for the Medal of Honor and took steps to see that no one deserving the highest award had been overlooked or given a lesser decoration. Five days after the Armistice he directed that a careful review be made of all cases in which a Distinguished Service Cross had been given, to see if a Medal of Honor should be awarded in its stead. Of the 98 Medals of Honor conferred for valor in action during World War I, 25 were given posthumously.

Three men from the 27th Division of the A.E.F. provide an example of the courage in action deemed worthy of the Medal of Honor. On September 29, 1918, that division formed the spearhead of the Allied armies facing the Hindenburg Line. After advancing under a murderous fire from the front and both flanks, which had all but destroyed the attacking Allied units, a group of men from the 27th—the third platoon of the 107th Machine Gun Company, under the command of Sergeant John C. Latham

—moved into a draw concealed by a smoke barrage. Not knowing how the battle was going to the right or left of them, Latham moved his men forward. When the smoke lifted he saw that they were far in advance of any friendly unit and appeared to be surrounded.

Looking through his field glasses to assess their situation, Latham spotted an American officer signaling for aid from about a hundred yards away. Near him was a disabled tank which the enemy was shelling with mortars, machine guns, and rifles. Latham, with Sergeant Alan Eggers and Corporal Thomas O'Shea, left his platoon and dashed through this rain of fire toward the tank. On the way O'Shea, carrying their machine gun, was killed and the gun destroyed. Latham and Eggers kept going. They reached the tank, removed from it a machine gun and all the ammunition they could carry, and led the officer and two other men they found near it—all wounded—back to cover. Latham set up the machine gun on the lip of a shell crater and got it firing just in time to turn back a German detachment sent out to storm their position.

Eggers and another man volunteered to go for help and left the crater. Wounded himself, Eggers rounded up the four remaining members of the platoon, also wounded, but they were pinned down by enemy fire and unable to get back to the large crater. Latham, meanwhile, manned the machine gun. Twice it jammed and twice the sergeant, with only a cartridge for a tool, cleared it and continued to defend the position. When night fell Eggers crept back to the crater, and he and Latham led the small party—by then consisting of sixteen men, eleven of whom were wounded—back to the Allied lines under cover of darkness, picking up more wounded on the way. Two days later, on the same battlefield, Latham was wounded in the side by a shell fragment, and spent ten weeks in a British field hospital.

Latham, Eggers, and O'Shea (the last posthumously) were awarded not only the Medal of Honor, but also, from Britain, the Distinguished Conduct Medal; from France, the Medaille Militaire and the Croix de Guerre with Palm; from Italy, the Cross of War; from Portugal, the War Cross; and from Montenegro, the

Medal of Bravery. Latham received his Medal of Honor from General Pershing himself, at Pershing's headquarters in Chaumont. He recalls that "Pershing shook my hand, looked me right in the eye, and said, 'I'd swap my stars for this medal. . . .' " Latham has never forgotten that moment.

Since 1917, 485 more names have been added to the list of those awarded the Army Medal of Honor, bringing the total to 2199. Of this number, 293 were still living in 1962 when Army installations throughout the world observed a Medal of Honor Centennial. The celebration extended from July 12, the date on which in 1862 Congress first authorized the Medal of Honor for the Army, to March 25, 1963. The latter date marked the hundredth anniversary of the occasion on which the Medal was first conferred, on six soldiers of the Union Army who in 1863 took part in a mission to sabotage a railroad behind the Confederate lines; with the railroad, which ran from Marietta, Georgia, to Chattanooga, Tennessee, out of commission, the entire state of Tennessee would have been cut off from the Confederacy. The mission failed, but the party that made the daring attempt was known as Mitchell's Raiders.

The medal is now awarded for action in the Vietnam conflict.

Navy

The Navy's Medal of Honor is older, in point of authorization, than the Army's. The award was created by an Act of Congress of December 21, 1861, seven months before the Army Medal was instituted. The provisions for the award have been amended several times, most recently in 1942.

The Medal of Honor is conferred by the Congress on any officer or enlisted man of the Navy or Marine Corps who shall, in action involving actual conflict with the enemy, distinguish himself conspicuously by gallantry and intrepidity at the risk of his life, above and beyond the call of duty. Unlike the Army Medal, the Navy's highest decoration was originally given for noncombat heroism as well; many early awards of the Medal were for lifesaving. A new form of the Medal was established after World War I, to be given for combat action only; but until 1942 the old form of the Medal was also in use, to recognize noncombat acts of conspicuous gallantry.

1862–1913

The design of the Navy Medal of Honor, by Christian Schussel, was accepted by Secretary of the Navy Gideon Welles in May 1862. The five-pointed bronze star, its obverse showing Minerva repulsing the figure of Discord, is identical with the original Army Medal of Honor, described on page 3. The reverse of the Navy medal is blank, except for the words "Personal Valor," below which were engraved the recipient's name, rank, and ship or organization, and the date of the action being honored.

The medal is suspended from the flukes of an anchor, fouled by a cable; the anchor is attached by a ring at the top to an open clasp of fasces, with a five-pointed star at the center. The suspension ribbon, like that of the Army Medal, is a blue field above thirteen vertical red and white stripes. The bar pin above is also an open clasp of fasces, but without the star.

1913–1919

In 1913 the ribbon on the Navy Medal of Honor was changed to light blue with thirteen white stars. In this later version (shown in color plate I, no. 6), the fouled anchor below the clasp was replaced by a plain one. Uniform regulations of the period provided that the Medal of Honor should be worn around the neck, on a ribbon of plain light blue, rather than pinned on the breast, and a bronze loop, concealed by the folds of the neck ribbon, eventually took the place of the suspension ribbon and clasps.

1917–1942

Commonly referred to as the "new" Medal of Honor, this form of the award was authorized by Congress on February 4, 1919, principally for Navy and Marine Corps members who had distinguished themselves in actual combat in World War I.

The medal, designed by Tiffany and Company, New York, is a gold cross pattée, superimposed on a wreath of laurel leaves; the arms of the cross each bear an anchor within a plain raised border. The octagonal medallion in the center shows an eagle, like that on the great seal of the United States, encircled by the words "United States Navy" and "1917-1918." The reverse of the medal is blank, except for a raised inscription "Awarded to" at the top. The ribbon, blue with thirteen white stars, is suspended from a gold bar, bearing the word "Valour" in block letters within a raised border.

The "new" Medal of Honor was given only once after World War I—to a Marine lieutenant, Christian F. Schilt, for a combat action in Nicaragua in 1927. Meanwhile the "old" Medal of Honor continued to be awarded for noncombat action; it was conferred during the same Nicaraguan compaign, of 1926-1933, on Marine Corporal Donald LeRoy Truesdell, for an act of heroism while on patrol but not in actual contact with the enemy.

1942–present

An Act of Congress of August 7, 1942, abolished the "new" Medal of Honor of 1919 and re-established the medal originally authorized in 1862, with certain modifications in the design. A ribbon suspension similar to the Army's was adopted, with a short piece of light blue ribbon folded into a square or rectangle, the traditional thirteen white stars displayed in its center, and this in turn attached to a light blue neck ribbon.

✠

Two instances from World War II will show the brand of heroism for which the Navy Medal of Honor is granted. One instance comes from the Coast Guard, a branch of the service which operates under the Navy in wartime, and whose members are entitled to the awards and decorations authorized for the Department of the Navy. Coast Guard personnel manned the Navy's assault craft in every important combat landing in the war, and it was in one of these actions that Signalman First Class Douglas Albert Munro won the Medal of Honor.

On Guadalcanal, during America's first offensive in the Pacific, a battalion of Marines was trapped by enemy forces at Point Cruz on September 27, 1942. Signalman Munro led a detachment of twenty-four Higgins boats to the area to evacuate these men. He got his boats up to the beach, under heavy fire, and then, while they were being loaded, placed his own small craft between the beachhead and the enemy in order to draw their fire. He was mortally wounded before the task of evacuation was completed; his dying words were "Did they get off?" His crew carried on until the last heavily loaded boat had cleared the beach. Munro, who undoubtedly saved many lives by his act, was awarded the Medal of Honor posthumously for extraordinary heroism and conspicuous gallantry in action.

The second instance is from the Navy's Submarine Service —the "silent service," as it is called. In June 1944, the submarine U.S.S. *Harder* and her skipper, Commander Samuel David Dealey, made submarine and naval warfare history. In four patrols, the *Harder* and Dealey had already sent eleven Japanese ships, totaling almost fifty thousand tons, to the bottom. On her fifth patrol, the *Harder* tackled an enemy convoy which was guarded by destroyers. According to the submariners' "book," enemy destroyers were poison, and a sub that spotted one was ordered to run. But Dealey knew the Japanese had a shortage of destroyers, and if their number could be cut down further the Japanese merchant ships would be at the mercy of the American subs. He therefore decided to throw away the "book." When one of the enemy destroyers heeled over and headed toward the *Harder,* Dealey gave the order to fire on her. The destroyer broke apart and slipped beneath the waves. Shortly after this the *Harder* sank another destroyer at short range with a direct hit amidships.

Dealey then set course for Tawi Tawi, where a Japanese fleet was anchored. Only six miles from the enemy base, he spotted two more destroyers and sank them both. The following day the *Harder* encountered a large hostile fleet. An enemy destroyer, sighting the submarine, left the pack and was making smoke toward the *Harder*. Dealey fired three bow shots at the destroyer before he crash dived, and seconds later the *Harder* felt the impact as the exploding ship passed over her.

Commander Dealey was recommended for the Medal of Honor for this patrol, in which, as his citation reads, "five vital Japanese destroyers [were] sunk in five short-range torpedo attacks." The award was conferred on him posthumously, for the U.S.S. *Harder* was lost at sea with all hands on August 24, 1944. Dealey, who also won four Navy Crosses and a Silver Star Medal for his outstanding courage and gallantry, became a legend in the Submarine Service. Not only did he rewrite the "book" on submarine tactics; after the war was over, it was found that the commander of the Combined Japanese Fleet believed that the actions performed by a single craft, Dealey's *Harder,* had been the work of a massive concentration of American submarines.

BREVET MEDAL

Marine Corps

During the Mexican War (1846-1848), the Civil War (1861-1865), the Spanish-American War (1898), the Philippine Insurrection (1899-1913), and the Boxer Rebellion in China (1900-1901), Brevet Commissions for Bravery in Action were conferred upon officers of the Marine Corps, in recognition of distinguished conduct and public service in the presence of the enemy. However, no medal or badge accompanied the Commission, and the distinction was often lost sight of, particularly after World War I, when many new decorations, awards, badges, and ribbons were conferred. Major General John A. Lejeune, Commandant of the Marine Corps from 1920 to 1929, believed that the Brevet Commission, as a mark of honor associated with the early history of the Marine Corps, should receive recognition commensurate with the honors of a later day; in April 1921 he recommended that an appropriate medal, badge, or ribbon be prescribed to be worn by those who hold a Brevet Commission.

His recommendation was acted upon, and a directive from the Secretary of the Navy dated June 7, 1921, authorized the Brevet Medal to be awarded to all those whose Brevet Commissions were confirmed by the Senate.

The medal, designed by Quartermaster Sergeant Joseph A. Burnett, U.S.M.C., under the direction of Quartermaster General, C. L. McCawley, U.S.M.C., is a bronze cross pattée, with a circular medallion in the center bearing, on the obverse, the word "Brevet" within an encircling inscription "United States Marine Corps." The reverse has the circular inscription "For Distinguished Conduct" and centered within it the words "In Presence of Enemy." A small Marine Corps emblem joins the cross to the ribbon, which is of dark red moiré, studded with thirteen white stars.

At the time of its authorization, the Brevet Medal was awarded to twenty-three officers, three of whom already held the Medal of

Honor. Among them was the legendary Smedley D. Butler, who had received his Brevet Commission for gallant action during the Boxer Rebellion in China. Commanding a company of Marines (although he was not yet twenty years old), Butler was wounded in the leg in the fight for Tientsin. He left the hospital with his wound still unhealed to lead his men in the march on the Imperial City of Peking. When the column was halted by the Great City Wall, Butler scaled the wall and forced the main gate so that the Marines could enter the city.

His subsequent career was equally spectacular. When trouble broke out in Nicaragua in 1912, he led a battalion to the relief of besieged Granada. In Mexico in 1914, Butler carried out a hazardous reconnaissance of Mexico City, disguised as a business-man, and then led his battalion in the assault on Vera Cruz. He was awarded the Medal of Honor for the latter action, and surprised the Navy by trying to give it back, on the grounds that he did not deserve it. In Haiti in 1915, he personally led the assault on Fort Rivière, the last bandit stronghold, which his superiors feared could not be taken with less than three thousand men. "Hell, sir," said Butler—or so it is reported—"I can take that place with a hundred of my people." He did exactly that, and for it he was awarded a second Medal of Honor, which he did not try to give back.

Sent to France in World War I, though not to combat, Butler was put in charge of Camp Pontnezen at Brest, the U.S. Army de-barkation center, which was disgracefully overcrowded and beset with flu. Of the 75,000 soldiers in the camp, 16,000 had the dreaded illness, and 250 died the day Butler assumed command. By working himself into exhaustion, he not only controlled the epi-demic but turned the camp into a show place where 106,000 troops were able to sleep between clean sheets and eat three hot meals a day. For this remarkable feat of organization Butler was awarded the Distinguished Service Medal, as well as the French Legion of Honor. When he retired in 1931, at the age of fifty, Butler was a major general and the holder of some fifteen decora-tions in addition to his two Medals of Honor and the Marine Corps Brevet Medal.

DISTINGUISHED SERVICE CROSS

Army

This decoration, second only to the Medal of Honor for Army personnel, was instituted by executive order on January 2, 1918, and confirmed by Congress on July 9, 1918. It is awarded to any person who, while serving in any capacity with the Army of the United States, shall have distinguished himself or herself by extraordinary heroism in connection with military operations against an armed enemy. It is awarded only for combat service.

The very striking design of the decoration was carried out by Captain Aymar Embury of the Army Engineer Reserve Corps. A sculptured inner cross on the obverse is mounted on a flat cross, with an ornamental scroll surmounted by a ball at the end of each arm. In the center of the cross is a laurel wreath, with an American eagle, wings spread and raised, upon it. At the eagle's feet is a scroll bearing the words "For Valor."

The reverse of the medal is also a sculptured inner cross on a flat cross with decorative ends; the back of the scroll and the tips of the eagle's wings are shown. A circular laurel wreath is joined in the center by a bowknot, within which is a blank space for the recipient's name. The ribbon is dark blue, with narrow white and red stripes at the edges.

First Style

A variation on the present form of the Distinguished Service Cross, called the "first" or "French" style, is sometimes seen, in which the arms of the cross are heavily ornamented with oak leaves; the eagle is mounted on a diamond-shaped plaque, and the scroll below it bears the words *"E Pluribus Unum."* Only about a hundred of this early form of the decoration were awarded.

The Distinguished Service Cross is awarded for acts such as that of a young infantry sergeant, Audie Murphy, during the landings in Normandy in World War II. Staff Sergeant Murphy, already a veteran of Sicily and Anzio, led a platoon of the 15th Infantry Regiment, Fourth Division, in the first wave that landed at Ramatuelle, France, on August 15, 1944.

When the platoon's advance inland was halted by intense enemy machine-gun and small-arms fire from a boulder-strewn hill ahead, Murphy ordered his men to take cover. He then dashed forty yards through withering fire to a draw, worked his way back to the beach, and formed a machine-gun squad. He returned and placed the machine gun seventy-five yards in advance of his platoon, in an exposed position, and in the duel that ensued managed to silence the enemy weapon, killing two of its crew and wounding a third. He then picked up the gun and advanced alone up the rocky hill, firing as he went. When two Germans advanced toward him, he quickly killed both. Another enemy machine gun opened up, and he sprayed it with fire until he ran out of ammunition. Then he took a carbine and continued, still alone, toward the German strongpoint. Closing in on the last enemy position, he wounded two Germans and killed two others in a fierce, brief exchange of fire. He then forced the remaining Germans to surrender. The citation that accompanied Murphy's award of the Distinguished Service Cross noted that "His extraordinary heroism resulted in the capture of a fiercely contested enemy-held hill and the annihilation or capture of the entire enemy garrison."

Audie Murphy was a second lieutenant at the end of the war. He had amassed twenty-three decorations and medals, including, in addition to the Distinguished Service Cross, the Medal of Honor, three Silver Stars, a Legion of Merit, a Bronze Star, and three Purple Hearts. The French government awarded him the Legion of Honor and the Croix de Guerre.

NAVY CROSS

The Navy Cross, second only to the Medal of Honor for Navy personnel, is awarded to officers and enlisted men of the Navy and Marine Corps who distinguish themselves by extraordinary heroism in military operations against an armed enemy.

Authorized by Congress on February 4, 1919, this award was originally the Navy's third highest decoration, and was given both for combat heroism and for other distinguished service. Although the greater number of the early awards were for service in World War I, a number of Navy Crosses were conferred for heroism in rescue and salvage operations during submarine disasters, as those to the divers William Badders and Thomas Eadie, both of whom also received the Medal of Honor for acts of gallantry in diving. An Act of Congress of August 7, 1942, gave the Navy Cross precedence over the Distinguished Service Medal, making it a combat award only, and giving it second place in the Navy's "pyramid of honor."

The decoration, designed by James E. Fraser, is a cross of dark bronze, with rounded ends; in each of the four re-entrant angles is a cluster of laurel and berries. The round medallion in the center shows on its obverse a sailing vessel—a caravel—seen from the side, and sailing to the left. The reverse of this center medallion shows crossed anchors joined at the top by a cable, with the letters "U" and "S" in the angles formed by the anchors, with the letter "N" centered below. A scroll at the top of the cross joins it to a ring suspended from the ribbon. The ribbon is navy blue, with a narrow white center stripe.

In Nicaragua in 1928, a young Marine captain, Merritt A. Edson, performed a deed of great daring which earned him the Navy Cross. Edson took ashore from the U.S.S. *Denver* a detachment of Marines, numbering about forty, to help quell an uprising led by the Nicaraguan bandit chief Sandino. Loading his men into tricky native boats, he led them some four hundred miles up the

Coco River to Sandino's jungle headquarters. After a brisk fire fight with Sandino's main force, Edson and his Marines drove off the defenders and reached Poteca, the bandits' stronghold. Sandino himself managed to escape, but Edson captured one of his colonels and a quantity of the bandits' supplies.

In reporting Edson's Coco River patrol to the Commandant of the Marine Corps, the area commander, Brigadier General Feland, wrote, "From the standpoint of difficulty, danger, isolation from friendly ground troops, and accomplishments, this small expedition is without parallel in the hard work done by this Brigade." Edson demonstrated the same qualities of leadership to a marked degree as commander of the First Marine Raiders during World War II, when his daring and courage won him the Medal of Honor for his action during the fight for Guadalcanal.

AIR FORCE CROSS

This decoration, established by Congress on July 6, 1960, as one of several awards created specifically for the Department of the Air Force, ranks second only to the Medal of Honor for Air Force personnel, thus taking the place of the Distinguished Service Cross. It is awarded to any person who, while serving in any capacity with the United States Air Force, shall have distinguished himself by extraordinary heroism in connection with military operations against an armed enemy. The award will be given for combat action only.

This striking decoration, designed by the United States Mint, is a sculptured straight cross with an American eagle in the center. Behind the eagle is a symbolic cloud, surrounded by a wreath of laurel. The reverse has a raised plaque on the vertical arm, for the recipient's name.

The ribbon is light blue, with narrow white and red stripes at each edge.

CERTIFICATE OF MERIT

Army

This may be considered our country's second oldest award for meritorious service. Established during the Mexican War by an Act of Congress of March 3, 1847, it was originally a certificate, to be awarded by the President of the United States to privates only, for gallantry in action or for specially meritorious service in time of peace. The certificate read, in part:

> Know all whom it may concern that ——, Company —— of the —— Regiment of ——, having distinguished himself in the services of the United States on the —— day of —— in the battle of ——, on the recommendation of ——, the Commanding Officer of the Regiment, I do hereby award to the said ——, this Certificate of Merit, which, under the provisions of the 17th section of the Act approved March 3d, 1847, entitles him to additional pay at the rate of two dollars per month.

The first award of the Certificate of Merit was to Private John R. Scott, Company B, Second Dragoons, for heroism at the battle of Cerro Gordo in 1847. A total of 545 men received Certificates of Merit for conspicuous military service during the Mexican War; had the Medal of Honor been in existence at that time, many of these men might have received it instead. In 1854 noncommissioned officers were also made eligible for the award.

The Certificate of Merit was also given in peacetime for acts of heroism such as saving life or property from fire, the sea, or floods at the risk of one's life, or for other services that, in the judgment of the President, were deserving of the award. The wording of the certificate was altered appropriately when given for noncombat service.

Certificate of Merit Medal, 1905–1918

On January 11, 1905, a medal was authorized to be worn by all holders of the Certificate of Merit and to be given thereafter

to any private soldier or noncommissioned officer "who shall distinguish himself by Merit and Courage" and whom the President deemed worthy of the award.

The circular medal, designed by Francis D. Millet, shows a bald eagle, very much like a Roman war eagle, standing on a baton, facing left. Around the outside is the inscription *"Virtutis et audaciae monumentum et praemium."* The reverse of the medal has the inscription "For Merit" in the center of a wreath of oak leaves, joined at the bottom by a bowknot. Outside the wreath the words "United States Army" form the upper part of a circle, completed at the bottom by thirteen stars. The ribbon has a narrow white stripe in the center, with broad stripes of red, white, and blue, of equal width, on either side.

The Certificate of Merit Medal had a rather short life, being discontinued in 1918 by a special Act of Congress of July 9. If holders of the medal so requested, upon surrender of their original Certificate of Merit Medal they were to be awarded a Distinguished Service Medal in its place. In 1934, this ruling was changed, and those whose Certificate of Merit Medals had been replaced by the Distinguished Service Medal were authorized to receive instead the Distinguished Service Cross. A total of 1211 enlisted members of the U.S. Army received the Certificate of Merit award during the seventy-one years in which it was conferred. It was never given to members of the naval services.

DISTINGUISHED SERVICE MEDAL

Army

This decoration, authorized by Presidential order on January 2, 1918, and confirmed by an Act of Congress of July 9, 1918, is awarded to any person who, while serving in any capacity with the Army of the United States after April 6, 1917, shall distinguish himself or herself by "exceptionally meritorious service to the government in a duty of great responsibility." It may be awarded for combat or noncombat service.

This decoration was designed—as was the Distinguished Service Cross—by Captain Aymar Embury of the Army Engineer Corps Reserve; the sculptor was Corporal Gaetano Cecere, U.S. Army. The medal pendant, of gold colored bronze, bears the coat of arms of the United States within a circle of dark blue enamel. On the enamel in the inscription, in gold, "For Distinguished Service." and "MCMXVIII." On the reverse is a circular arrangement of flags and weapons, with a scroll left blank for the recipient's name. The pendant is attached to the ribbon by a swivel and an ornamented bar. The ribbon has a wide white center stripe, flanked on either side by a narrow blue stripe with a broad scarlet stripe at the edge.

The first awards of the Distinguished Service Medal for service in World War I were to the commanding officers of the Allied armies. The medal was conferred at the direction of the President of the United States on Marshals Foch and Joffre and General Pétain of France; Field Marshal Haig of Great Britain; General Díaz of Italy; General Gillain of Belgium; and our own General Pershing. The award was given on October 21, 1918, to "General John Joseph Pershing, Commanding General, Allied Expeditionary Force, as a token of the gratitude of the American people to the commander of our armies in the field for his distinguished services," as the citation read, and "in appreciation of the success which our armies have achieved under his leadership."

Navy

The Navy's Distinguished Service Medal, authorized by an Act of Congress of February 4, 1919, as amended on August 7, 1942, is awarded to any person who, while serving with the Navy of the United States in any capacity, since April 6, 1917, shall have distinguished himself by exceptionally meritorious service to the government in a duty of great responsibility. It may be awarded for combat or noncombat service.

The medal, designed by Paul Manship, is of gilded bronze, circular in shape with a decorative suspension. An American eagle is shown on the obverse, standing with wings spread and gripping in its talons an olive branch and arrows. A circle of blue enamel bears the words "United States of America" and "Navy" in gold; outside it is a gold border in a wave pattern. This pendant hangs from a white five-pointed star, each point tipped with a gold ball; in the center of the star is a gold anchor, and gold rays are seen in the re-entrant angles.

The reverse of the medal is bordered with the same gold scroll or wave pattern; on the inner circle of blue enamel is the inscription, in gold, "For Distinguished Service." Within a wreath of laurel is Neptune's trident. The reverse of the white star above is plain. The ribbon is navy blue with a narrow center stripe of gold, these being the Navy's colors.

First Style: An earlier design of the Distinguished Service Medal is sometimes seen, though it was never authorized for award. Designed by the jewelry firm of Whitehead and Hoag, it is circular in shape. A large anchor with a rope coiled around it is seen in the center foreground. In the background are waves, and on the horizon to the left is the setting sun. At the bottom right, behind the fluke of the anchor, is a spray of laurel. Across the top are the words "Distinguished Service." The suspension is in the form of an eagle, whose wings are spread so that the tips extend beyond the outer edges of the ribbon. At the eagle's feet is a scroll bearing the dates "1917–1918." The ribbon is the same as in the design described above.

✠

Admiral William Frederick Halsey, Jr., of the United States Navy, one of the most outstanding fighting men ever to wear the blue and gold, was presented with the Navy's Distinguished Service Medal for his part in the first naval offensive against the Japanese in the Pacific in World War II. As commander of the Marshall Raiding Force of the Pacific Fleet, Halsey was commended, in the citation that accompanied the medal, "especially for his brilliant and audacious attack against the Marshall and Gilbert Islands on January 31, 1942. By his great skill and determination, this drive inflicted heavy damage to enemy ships and planes."

The campaign in the Marshalls was only the beginning for Admiral Halsey. The B-25s that carried out the first bombing raid on Japan were launched from his flagship, in a daring operation that took him within five hundred miles of the Japanese mainland in April 1942. In 1943 he commanded the U.S. Naval Forces in the battle of Bougainville. In June 1944 he was made commander of the U.S. Third Fleet, and with his fleet supported the landing on Leyte Island in the Philippines, the landing on Luzon, and, in the closing months of the war, the bombing of the Japanese home islands. In December 1945 Halsey was promoted to the rank of five-star admiral of the fleet, in token of the leading part he had played in the defeat of Japan.

Coast Guard

The Distinguished Service Medal, authorized for the Coast Guard in 1951 (the design was not approved until 1962), is the highest decoration awarded exclusively to that service, and is to replace the Navy Distinguished Service Medal, until now awarded Coast Guard personnel. For the Coast Guard it ranks second only to the Medal of Honor for combat action and is its highest decoration for noncombat service.

The gold circular medal has in its center a sailing ship of the cutter class under full sail, representing the *Massachusetts,* the first ship of the Revenue Cutter Service, organized in 1790, which was the forerunner of the Coast Guard. A raised circle surrounds the ship, and between this and the raised outer rim of the medal are the words "U.S. Coast Guard" and "Distinguished Service."

The reverse of the medal bears the Coast Guard seal, which is the shield of the United States with the words *"Semper"* above it and *"Paratus"* below, within the circular inscription "United States Coast Guard 1790." The seal is centered upon two broad crossed anchors, with a curved ribbon design below left blank for the recipient's name. The ribbon is blue, with a narrow white and a broad purple stripe on either side.

Air Force

This decoration, established by Congress on July 6, 1960, as one of several Air Force awards, takes the place of the Army Distinguished Service Medal previously awarded Air Force personnel. It is conferred on any person who, while serving in any capacity with the U.S. Air Force, shall have distinguished himself by exceptionally meritorious service to the government in a duty of great responsibility. It may be given for combat or noncombat achievements. The medal itself is still in the development stage, and no further details about it are available.

SILVER STAR MEDAL

Army

The Silver Star Medal had its beginning during World War I. An Act of Congress of July 9, 1918, authorized the wearing by Army personnel of a small silver star, $\frac{3}{16}$ of an inch in diameter, upon the service ribbon of a campaign medal, to indicate "a citation for gallantry in action, published in orders issued from headquarters of a general officer, not warranting the award of a Medal of Honor or Distinguished Service Cross." Known in the Army as the "citation star," the award was made retroactive, so that all those cited for gallantry in action in previous campaigns, even as far back as the Spanish-American War, were eligible to wear it. It was estimated that more than 20,000 men had received such citations before 1918.

On August 8, 1932, the Silver Star Medal was established by an Act of Congress. This medal, designed by Bailey, Banks and Biddle, is gilt bronze in the shape of a star 1¼ inches from point to point. In the center of the obverse is a plain laurel wreath; within this is a silver star, the same size as the original citation star, from which rays extend to the inner edges of the wreath. The reverse of the medal is inscribed "For Gallantry in Action," below which is a space left blank for the recipient's name.

Originally the medal was suspended from the ribbon by a ring that went through the upper point of the star. The current suspension is square and is of a piece with the medal itself. The ribbon, one of the most striking of all American decoration ribbons, has a red center stripe flanked on either side by white, blue, thin white, and thin blue stripes.

Navy

The Silver Star Medal was not authorized for the Navy until August 7, 1942, when an Act of Congress also authorized two dollars a month additional pay, from the date of the act cited, for each man who received the award. Those in the naval service at that time who had previously been recommended for the Medal of Honor, the Navy Cross, or the Distinguished Service Medal, but whose recommendation had not been approved, were awarded the Silver Star.

The medal itself is the same for both services.

✠

Corporal Alfred J. Abbott was one of those awarded the Silver Star for conspicuous gallantry and intrepidity in action in the Korean War. He was part of the Second Battalion of the First Marine Division, which on September 21, 1950, was poised to attack Yongdungpo, called the "key to Seoul," in its drive up through South Korea after the landings at Inchon.

As one of the fire-team leaders of Fox Company, Corporal Abbott, when the assault was ordered at 0630 on the 21st, moved his men forward in the face of heavy machine-gun and small-arms fire. The corporal led the attack personally, wiping out with hand grenades and deadly effective rifle fire an enemy machine-gun nest, its gunners, and the rifleman protecting it.

When his fire-team was forced to seek cover, because of the intensity of the enemy fire, Abbott, although wounded, carried out a one-man assault on the heavily fortified hostile position. Hit again and again, blinded by grenade shrapnel, he collapsed while still moving forward, but his magnificent action was an inspiration to the Marines, who charged up the hill, and, after a brief bitter fight, drove the enemy off and secured this vital position.

The citation for which Abbott was tendered the Silver Star commends his "courageous initiative, leadership and devotion to duty" and praises him for "upholding the highest traditions of the United States Naval Service."

LEGION OF MERIT

The Legion of Merit, the first United States decoration created specifically for award to citizens of other nations, was established by an Act of Congress of July 20, 1942, amended by an executive order of March 15, 1955. It is conferred on officers and enlisted men of the armed forces of the United States and on nationals of other countries "who shall have distinguished themselves by exceptionally meritorious conduct in the performance of outstanding services" since September 8, 1939, the date of the President's proclamation of the state of emergency that led to World War II. The Legion of Merit may be awarded for combat or noncombat services; in the case of American military personnel, if the award is for combat service it is shown by the wearing of a combat "V."

The Legion of Merit was originally ranked directly below the Distinguished Service Medal in the Navy's "pyramid of honor." This was changed by Navy directive number 49 of January 28, 1946, which placed the Legion of Merit immediately below the Silver Star, thus making it the Navy's fifth ranking decoration.

The Legion of Merit is also the first award to have different degrees. If a holder of the Legion of Merit in one degree is subsequently given another such award, it is never in a degree lower than the original one. The degrees of Chief Commander and Commander are conferred on members of foreign governments only and are awarded for services comparable to those for which the Distinguished Service Medal is given to members of the United States armed forces.

The degrees (in descending order) are as follows:

Chief Commander

This is awarded to chiefs of state or heads of government of foreign countries. One of the first recipients was Generalissimo Chiang Kai-shek, who was cited for "extraordinary fidelity and exceptional military conduct in the performance of outstanding services."

The Chief Commander's Legion of Merit is a large breast plate, designed—as were all the degrees of this decoration—by Colonel Townsend Heard, U.S.A.; the sculptor for all was Katharine W. Lane. It is a five-pointed star, its V-shaped extremities each tipped with a gold ball. The star is enamel, white bordered in purplish-red, rimmed with gold. In the center is a blue enamel field with thirteen white stars, the whole encircled by clouds of gold. The stars are arranged in the pattern that appears on the United States coat of arms, representing "the new constellation," i.e., the new Republic. The white enamel star is superimposed on a laurel wreath of green enamel, joined at the bottom by a gold bowknot. In the angles of the star, within the wreath, are crossed arrows pointing outward. The reverse of the badge has engraved in its center the words "United States of America." A miniature of the star, in gold on a small horizontal gold bar, is worn on the ribbon.

Commander

This is awarded to the foreign equivalent of a chief of staff in the United States military hierarchy or to a leader of comparable degree lower than a chief of state.

The badge is a star similar to the Chief Commander's, but slightly smaller, and worn around the neck. In the V-shaped angle at the top of the star is a bronze laurel wreath, with an oval ring above it through which the neck ribbon passes. On the reverse, the arms of the star are enameled in white and purplish-red, as on the obverse, but the laurel wreath, in green on the obverse, appears on the reverse as a scroll with the words "United States of America" in gold. Above a blank space in the center of the star are the words *"Annuit Coeptis"* (He [God] has favored our undertakings), a motto from the Great Seal, with the date "MDCCLXXXII," 1782—the year of the first United States decoration, the Badge of Military Merit, from which the present Purple Heart derives (see page 63). A miniature silver replica of the star on a small silver horizontal bar is worn on the ribbon bar.

Officer

This is awarded to generals or flag rank personnel below the equivalent of a United States military chief of staff and to ranks comparable to colonel or captain in the naval forces, for service in assignments equivalent to those normally carried out by generals or flag rank personnel in the armed forces of the United States; and to foreign military attachés.

The medal is again the same as in the Commander's badge, but slightly smaller. In the more recent awards of this degree, there has been no enamel on the reverse of the medal. The wreath suspension at the top of the star, as in the Commander's badge, is replaced by a large loop suspension. A miniature replica of the star in gold is worn on the suspension ribbon (see color plate IV, no. 7) and also on the ribbon bar.

Legionnaire

This badge is awarded to all others eligible for the Legion of Merit. The medal has the same size, shape, and design as those of the officer's badge, but the replica of the star is not worn on the ribbon.

The ribbon for all degrees is of purplish-red moiré with a narrow white stripe at either edge.

DISTINGUISHED FLYING CROSS

This medal is awarded to any officer or enlisted man of the armed forces of the United States who shall have distinguished himself by "heroism or extraordinary achievement while participating in an aerial flight, subsequent to November 11, 1918." The decoration may also be given for an act performed prior to November 11, 1918, when the individual has been recommended for, but has not received the Medal of Honor, Distinguished Service Cross, Navy Cross, or Distinguished Service Medal.

The Distinguished Flying Cross, authorized by an Act of Congress of July 2, 1926 (amended by Executive Order 7786 on January 8, 1938), was awarded first to Captain Charles A. Lindbergh, of the U.S. Army Corps Reserve, for his solo flight of 3600 miles across the Atlantic in 1927, a feat which electrified the world and made "Lindy" one of America's most popular heroes. The first D.F.C. to be awarded to a Navy man was to Commander Richard E. Byrd, of the U.S. Navy Air Corps, on May 9, 1926, for his exciting flight to and from the North Pole. Both these famous aviators also received the Medal of Honor with the Distinguished Flying Cross. The aviatrix Amelia Earhart also received the Distinguished Flying Cross. Hers was the only such award, as an executive order of March 1, 1927, ruled that the D.F.C. should not be conferred on civilians.

During wartime, members of the armed forces of friendly foreign nations serving with the United States are eligible for the D.F.C. It is also given to those who display heroism while working as instructors or students at flying schools.

The medal, which is identical for all branches of the service, is a bronze cross pattée. On the obverse is a four-bladed propeller, one blade in each arm of the cross; in the re-entrant angles of the cross are rays which form a square. The reverse of the medal is left blank for the recipient's name and deed. The cross is suspended by a rectangular-shaped bar, in the center of which is a plain shield, from a ribbon having a red center stripe, flanked on

either side by a narrow white stripe, a wide blue, a white, and, at the edges, a blue stripe.

Subsequent awards of the Distinguished Flying Cross are indicated by the oak-leaf clusters for Army and Air Force personnel and by additional-award stars for all other services.

Noncombat Medals

SOLDIER'S MEDAL

This medal, authorized by an Act of Congress of July 2, 1926, the same as that which established the Distinguished Flying Cross, is awarded to any person who, while serving in any capacity with the United States Army, National Guard, or Organized Reserves shall distinguish himself or herself by "heroism not involving actual conflict with an armed enemy." The act of heroism must have meant personal hazard or danger and the voluntary risk of life. Usually the degree of heroism required is the same as that for the Distinguished Flying Cross.

The medal, designed by Gaetano Cecere, is octagonal. An eagle, wings upraised, perched on a fasces, is displayed on the obverse, with six stars and a spray of leaves above on its right and seven stars on its left. The reverse of the medal has in its center a shield paly of thirteen sections, with the letters "U.S." on the largest. To the left of the shield are sprays of laurel and to the right sprays of oak, joined by a scroll that passes behind the shield. The upper edge of the medal is inscribed "Soldier's Medal." Near the bottom are the words "For Valor" above a plaque left blank for the recipient's name. The ribbon consists of alternating narrow white and red stripes, seven of white and six of red, in the center, flanked by a wide blue stripe at either edge.

In early May of 1961, the raging Twin Forks River, in Kentucky, flooded its banks and caught many people in their homes. Army units from nearby Fort Knox were dispatched to the scene to aid in rescue attempts. About fifteen miles south of Louisville, a rescue team of the 90th Transportation Company (Medium Helicopter) spotted a house in which two elderly people were trapped. Tall trees and electric wires made any attempt to rescue them hazardous.

Sergeant First Class William W. Heiden, flight engineer of an H-37 helicopter, volunteered to try to get them out. He was lowered down a seventy-five-foot cable onto the roof of the house, with full knowledge that one gust of wind could easily cause his death by slamming him into the trees or electric wires. Using his hands and feet, he succeeded in tearing and kicking a large hole in the slippery roof, through which he was able to lift the man and his wife, who by this time had moved into the attic of the house because of the rapidly rising water. Despite the further hazard of a hundred-knot downwash from the helicopter, Heiden managed to secure harnesses on the panic-stricken couple and they were raised safely into the aircraft. His courageous action and his selfless regard for his personal safety, which resulted in the saving of two lives, won Heiden the Soldier's Medal on October 9, 1961.

NAVY AND MARINE CORPS MEDAL

This medal, authorized by Congress on August 7, 1942, is awarded to anyone who, while serving with the Navy or the Marine Corps, including their Reserves, shall since December 6, 1941, have distinguished himself or herself by heroism not involving actual conflict with the enemy; it is also conferred on any person previously awarded a letter of commendation by the Secretary of the Navy for heroism not involving combat, regardless of the date of such a deed.

The medal, one of the most distinctive to come out of World War II, was designed by Lt. Commander McClelland Barclay, U.S.N.R., a well-known artist who was reported missing in action off New Georgia Island before his design was accepted. The obverse of the octagon-shaped medal pictures an eagle with wings spread, facing left, perched on an anchor below which is shown a globe of the world with the inscription "Heroism" beneath it. The reverse has a blank space for the recipient's name. The ribbon is navy blue, gold, and scarlet, in stripes of equal width, representing the Navy's blue and gold and the Marine Corps' scarlet and gold colors.

President John F. Kennedy was awarded the Navy and Marine Corps Medal for an act of heroism during World War II. This award was conferred on the President, then a lieutenant j.g. in the U.S.N.R., rather than a combat award, because the enemy had broken off contact with his sinking ship when the deed for which he was decorated took place. The citation accompanying his award of the medal read:

> For extremely heroic conduct as Commanding Officer of Motor Torpedo Boat 109, following the collision and sinking of that vessel in the Pacific War Area on August 1-2, 1943. Unmindful of personal danger, Lieutenant Junior Grade Kennedy unhesitatingly braved the difficulties and hazards of darkness to direct rescue operations, swimming many hours to secure aid and food after he had succeeded in getting his crew ashore. His outstanding courage, endurence, and leadership contributed to the saving of several lives and was in keeping with the highest traditions of the United States Naval Service.

COAST GUARD MEDAL

This medal is awarded by the Secretary of the Treasury, for the President but not in the name of Congress, to any person serving in any capacity with the Coast Guard who shall distinguish himself by heroism not involving actual conflict with the enemy. The individual must have performed a voluntary act of courage surpassing normal expectation and in the face of great danger to himself. For Coast Guard personnel the award takes precedence over the Distinguished Flying Cross.

Though authorized in 1951, the Coast Guard medal was not struck until 1958. It is octagonal, as are the other noncombat medals pictured above, and bears on its obverse the Coast Guard seal—the shield of the United States with the words "Semper" above and "Paratus" below, within a ring bearing the inscription "United States Coast Guard 1790," this in turn being centered on two broad crossed anchors. The seal is enclosed within a circle of rope. The reverse is plain except for the inscription "For Heroism," below which is engraved the recipient's name. The ribbon is medium blue in the center and at either edge, with

two stripes, each consisting of four white and three red narrow bands.

The Coast Guard medal was first awarded in October 1958 to two Coast Guardsmen who in August 1957 had attempted the rescue of three construction workers trapped 5800 feet under Lake Ontario, after an explosion in the waterworks tunnel at Oswego, New York. Engineman Third Class Earl H. Leyda and Boatswain's Mate Third Class Raymond A. Johnson volunteered to try to reach these men, and at great risk of their own lives they did so, though they were too late to find the workers alive.

AIRMAN'S MEDAL

This decoration, one of several Air Force awards established by Congress on July 6, 1960, takes the place of the Soldier's Medal for Air Force personnel. It is awarded to any member of the armed forces of the United States or of a friendly nation who, while serving in any capacity with the United States Air Force after the date of the award's authorization, shall have distinguished himself or herself by a heroic act, usually at the voluntary risk of his or her life but not involving actual combat.

The circular medal has on its obverse the figure of the Greek god Hermes in his winged cap; resting on one knee, he has just released from his open hands a falcon, shown rising into flight. Within the raised rim of the medal is the raised inscription, "Airman's Medal." The reverse, also with a raised rim, bears the inscription "For Valor" above a space for the recipient's name, within a stylized laurel wreath open at the top and tied at the bottom. The ribbon has alternating stripes, seven yellow and six dark blue, in the center, flanked by wide light-blue stripes.

The Airman's Medal is unusual in that it does not have the octagonal shape of its counterparts, the Soldier's Medal, the Navy and Marine Corps Medal, and the Coast Guard Medal. It had been established practice heretofore to design military decorations with a distinctive shape, so that they would not be confused at a distance with the service medals, which are always circular.

BRONZE STAR MEDAL

This decoration, authorized by Executive Order No. 9419 on February 4, 1944, is awarded a person in any branch of the military service who, while serving in any capacity with the armed forces of the United States on or after December 7, 1941, shall have distinguished himself by heroic or meritorious achievement or service, not involving participation in aerial flight, in connection with military operations against an armed enemy.

The award recognizes acts of heroism performed in ground combat if they are of lesser degree than that required for the Silver Star. It also recognizes single acts of merit and meritorious service if the achievement or service is of a lesser degree than that deemed worthy of the Legion of Merit; but such service must have been accomplished with distinction.

Army personnel who, as members of the armed forces of the United States between December 7, 1941, and September 2, 1945, were awarded the Combat Infantryman's Badge or Medical Badge for exemplary conduct may upon application receive the Bronze Star Medal. Although these World War II badges were not authorized for award until after July 1, 1943, those whose meritorious achievements in combat before that date can be confirmed in writing may also be eligible for the Bronze Star Medal.

The medal, designed by the firm of Bailey, Banks and Biddle, is in the shape of a five-pointed star 1½ inches from point to point. In its center is a smaller raised star. The small star is set on a raised ten-pointed figure, from which rays extend to the points of the outer star, giving the whole a sculptured effect. The reverse of the medal also has a raised center, with rays extending to the five points of the star. Inscribed on this are the words "Heroic or Meritorious Achievement," encircling a blank space for the recipient's name. The ribbon is predominantly red, with a narrow blue center stripe flanked on either side by a narrow white stripe, and a narrow white stripe at the outer edge. A bronze "V" on the ribbon denotes combat service.

AIR MEDAL

This award, established on May 11, 1942, by Executive Order 9158 and amended by Executive Order 9242-A, on September 11, 1942, is given to any person who, while serving with the armed forces of the United States in any capacity subsequent to September 8, 1939, shall have distinguished himself by meritorious achievement while participating in aerial flight. It is given for combat or noncombat action, and may be conferred in recognition of single acts of merit or of sustained operational activities against an armed enemy of the United States.

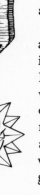

The decoration, which is identical for all branches of the armed forces, was designed by Walker K. Hancock. The medal is in the form of a 16-point sculptured compass rose of bronze. In the center of the rose on the obverse is an American eagle volant in the attitude of attack; gripped in its talons are flashes of lightning. The reverse has a raised circular disk on the compass rose, left blank for the recipient's name. The top of the rose has a decorative pointer to which a ring is attached. The ribbon which passes through this ring is medium blue, with a narrow golden-orange stripe on either side.

LIFE SAVING MEDALS

On June 20, 1874, Congress authorized two Life Saving Medals, one of gold and one of silver—denoting different degrees of heroism—to be awarded to persons who rescue or endeavor to rescue others from drowning, shipwreck, or other peril of the water. The rescue must have taken place within United States waters or in those subject to United States jurisdiction; or, if it occurs outside such waters, one of the parties must be a citizen of the United States.

The medals were authorized originally for award to military personnel; however, members of the armed forces are not at present recommended for Life Saving Medals unless a military decoration is considered wholly inappropriate. The Soldier's Medal, the Navy and Marine Corps Medal, or the Coast Guard Medal is given in most instances to members of the respective services for outstanding acts of heroism in saving or attempting to save individuals from drowning. Though the Life Saving Medals are now conferred chiefly on civilians, the administrative responsibility for their award rests with the Commandant of the U.S. Coast Guard. Since the Coast Guard in peacetime is an adjunct of the Treasury Department, the medals are known as "Treasury Department Life Saving Medals."

The original Life Saving Medals were large, 1⅝ inches in diameter; the gold medal hung from a ruby red ribbon and the silver medal from one of light blue. Both the size of the medals and the color of the suspension ribbons were amended by Congress on August 4, 1949. The present-day medals follow the design of the originals, but are smaller, more nearly the size of other such decorations.

Gold Medal

If the rescue or attempted rescue for which the Life Saving Medal is given has been made at the risk of the rescuer's own life, and

evidences extreme and heroic daring, the gold medal is conferred.

This medal, designed by Anthony C. Paquet, engraver of the original Medal of Honor, is 99.9 per cent pure gold. On the obverse three men are pictured in a small boat in a heavy sea. One is rescuing a man clinging to a spar, at the end of which is a block and line. Another is standing prepared to heave a line, and the third is rowing. In the distance to the left is the wreck of a vessel. A beaded circle surrounds this scene, and between it and the outer edge of the medal, in the upper half, is the inscription "United States of America." In the lower half are the words "Act of Congress August 4, 1949" in raised letters. (The original medal, of the larger size, bore the words "Act of Congress, June 20, 1874.") The medal hangs from a swivel, above which is an eagle, through whose wings the ribbon passes. The swivel is grasped in the eagle's beak.

The reverse of the medal has, in its center, a monument surmounted by an American eagle with wings spread. To the left and front of the monument stands a female figure, holding an oak wreath in her left hand while with her right she prepares to inscribe the name of the recipient in a blank space on the monument. To the right are grouped a ship's mast with sail, an anchor, a sextant, and a laurel branch. The whole is enclosed in a beaded circle, beween which and the raised outer edge is the inscription "In Testimony of Heroic Deeds in Saving Life from the Perils of the Sea." Centered at the bottom is a knot design. The ribbon has a wide gold center with a narrow white stripe and a broad red stripe at either end.

Silver Medal

If the rescue or attempted rescue for which the Life Saving Medal is awarded is not sufficiently distinguished to deserve the medal in gold, but evidences—in the wording of the 1874 authorization—"the exercise of such single exertion as to merit recognition," the silver medal is given.

This medal too was designed by Anthony C. Paquet, and is 99 per cent pure silver. The obverse shows the symbolic figure of a woman hovering over a man struggling in a heavy sea; the man is reaching for the end of a long scarf, which the woman extends to him with her right hand. A beaded circle surrounds this, between which and the outer raised edge of the medal is the inscription "United States of America" in the upper half, and the words "Act of Congress August 4, 1949" (or "Act of Congress June 20, 1874" in the case of the original medal) in the lower half. This medal, like the gold, is suspended by a swivel from the head of an eagle, through whose wings the ribbon passes.

The reverse of the medal bears a laurel wreath, whose center is left blank for the recipient's name. A beaded circle surrounds this, and between it and the raised outer edge is the inscription "In Testimony of Heroic Deeds in Saving Life from the Perils of the Sea.'" At the bottom is a decorative knot design. The ribbon is silver gray in the center, with a narrow white and a broad blue stripe on either side.

Additional Award Bars: A person may not receive more than one silver and one gold Life Saving Medal, but he may be awarded, in lieu of a succeeding award of the same class, a gold or silver bar. These are plain horizontal bars, 1⅝ inches long and 3/16 inch wide, composed of either gold or silver, depending on which medal has been awarded the recipient. A wide flowing ribbon, sculpted in the metal, is draped over the left end of the bar, passes in back of it, and reappears below. The part of the ribbon showing below the bar bears the inscription "Act of Congress August 4, 1949" (or "Act of Congress, June 20, 1874") in raised block letters. The bar and the ribbon are superimposed on a spray of laurel, the leaves of which show above and below.

COMMENDATION MEDAL

Army

This decoration—originally only a ribbon—was authorized in 1945 by War Department Circular 377; the metal pendant was not authorized until 1949. The award is given to any member of the armed forces of the United States who, while serving in any capacity with the Army on or after December 7, 1941, shall have distinguished himself or herself, either in combat or non-combat action, by meritorious achievement or meritorious service. The award may be made, upon application, to individuals who were commended on or after December 7, 1941, and prior to January 1, 1946, in a letter, certificate, or order of commendation (not a letter of appreciation) signed by an officer of the rank of major general or higher, for meritorious achievement or service performed subsequent to December 7, 1941. Individuals awarded a Commendation Ribbon prior to October 1, 1949, are, upon application, issued the Commendation Medal.

The medal pendant, designed by the Heraldic Branch of the Army's Quartermaster Corps, is a bronze hexagon, with one point up. In the center of the obverse is an American bald eagle, facing left, its wings displayed and grasping three crossed arrows, points to the left, in its talons. The wing tips extend to the outer edge of the medal. Upon the eagle's breast is a shield paly of thirteen sections and a chief.

The reverse of the medal bears the words "For Military," set in two lines, with a wide panel for the recipient's name centered below them, and under this the word "Merit." At the bottom is a sprig of laurel, pointing left. The ribbon has alternating narrow stripes, five of white and four of green, flanked on either side by a wide green stripe, with a narrow white stripe at the edge. A bronze "V" is worn on the ribbon to denote that the award is a combat decoration.

Only one Commendation Medal may be awarded to any individual. A second or succeeding award is indicated by a star worn on the ribbon.

Navy

Any officer or enlisted man of the Navy, Marine Corps, or Coast Guard who shall have received a letter of commendation signed by the Secretary of the Navy, by the Commander-in-Chief of the U.S. Fleet, Pacific, or the Atlantic Fleet, or by the Commanding General of the Fleet Marine Force, Pacific, for an act of service, combat or noncombat, performed between December 6, 1941, and January 11, 1944, is automatically authorized to wear the Navy Commendation Ribbon established on January 11, 1944. As in the case of the corresponding Army award, the medal pendant now worn was not authorized until March 22, 1950, by a directive from the Secretary of the Navy.

Personnel of the Navy, Marine Corps, and Coast Guard who shall have received such a commendation, signed by the Secretary of the Navy or one of the other designated authorities, after January 11, 1944, are authorized to wear the medal provided the letter of commendation specifically accords this privilege.

The medal pendant of the Navy Commendation award is identical with that of the Army decoration pictured on the opposite page; the ribbon is green, with a narrow white stripe near either edge (see color plate IV, no. 13). The combat "V" is worn on the ribbon if so stipulated in the citation. A star is authorized to denote a second or succeeding award.

Coast Guard

This award, originally only a ribbon, was authorized by the Secretary of the Treasury on August 26, 1947; the medal pendant was not authorized until July 5, 1951. The medal is awarded by the Secretary of the Treasury, or by the Commandant of the Coast Guard, to any member of the armed forces of the United States serving in any capacity with the Coast Guard, for meritorious service resulting in unusual and outstanding achievement rendered while the Coast Guard is under the Treasury Department's jurisdiction (that is, during peacetime).

The hexagonal pendant has on the obverse, within a circle simulating rope, an American bald eagle facing left, wings arched,

grasping in its right talon an olive branch and in its left a bunch of arrows. On the eagle's breast is a shield of crossed anchors, with the circular inscription "United States Coast Guard 1790" upon it; within the circle is the seal of the Treasury Department. The reverse of the medal has a blank plaque for the recipient's name, with the words "For Outstanding" above and "Service" below. Under this are three stars, the whole design being encircled by a laurel wreath and rope. The ribbon is green with a narrow white center stripe and a wider white stripe near either edge.

Air Force

This medal was authorized by the Secretary of the Air Force on March 28, 1958, for award to members of the armed forces of the United States who, while serving in any capacity with the Air Force after March 24, 1958, shall have distinguished themselves by meritorious achievement and service. The degree of merit must be distinctive, though it need not be unique. Acts of courage which do not involve the voluntary risk of life required for the Soldier's Medal (or the Airman's Medal now authorized for the Air Force) may be considered for the Commendation award.

The medal is a bronze hexagon, with one point up, centered upon which is the seal of the Air Force, an eagle with wings spread, facing left, perched upon a baton. There are clouds in the background. Below the seal is a shield bearing a pair of flyer's wings and a vertical baton with an eagle's claw at either end; behind the shield are eight lightning bolts.

The reverse of the medal is the same as that of the Army Commendation Medal, with the words "For Military Merit" below a panel for the recipient's name. The ribbon has a broad blue center stripe, flanked by a narrow yellow, a narrow blue, a very wide yellow, and finally a blue stripe.

PURPLE HEART

This award, the modern form of the original Purple Heart established by General George Washington in 1782 (page 63), is conferred on any person wounded in action while serving with the armed forces of the United States. It is also awarded posthumously to the next of kin of personnel killed or having died of wounds received in action after April 5, 1917.

The Purple Heart is awarded for combat action only. Prior to the adoption of the Legion of Merit and Bronze Star Medal, it was given by the Army for meritorious service. The decoration was authorized for the Army by a War Department order of February 22, 1932, and for Navy and Marine Corps personnel by a Navy Department order of January 21, 1943, superseded by an executive order of November 12, 1952.

The heart-shaped medal, one of the best known and also one of the most beautiful of our decorations, was designed by Elizabeth Will and modeled by John R. Sinnock. The inner heart on the obverse is of purple plastic (originally enamel), and the sculptured outer heart of gold-colored metal. On the purple heart General Washington is shown in profile, facing left, in a relief also of gold-colored metal. Above this heart is Washington's coat of arms, an enamel shield of white with two horizontal bands of red, and above them three red stars with sprays of green leaves on either side of the shield.

The reverse of the medal is entirely of gold-colored metal, including the shield and leaves. Within the sculptured outer heart and below the shield is the inscription, set in three lines, "For Military Merit," with a space below for the recipient's name. The ribbon is deep purple with narrow white edges.

Second and subsequent awards of the Purple Heart are denoted by a gold star for Navy and Marine Corps personnel and by an oak-leaf cluster for Army and Air Force personnel.

DISTINGUISHED UNIT CITATION

Army

This award, authorized by Executive Order 9075 on February 26, 1942, as superseded by Executive Order 9396 on December 2, 1943, is conferred on units of the armed forces of the United States and of cobelligerent nations, for extraordinary heroism in action against an armed enemy on or after December 7, 1941. The unit must display such gallantry, determination, and *esprit de corps* in accomplishing its mission as to set it apart from and above other units participating in the same campaign. The degree of heroism required is the same as that which would warrant the award of a Distinguished Service Cross to an individual.

An individual assigned or permanently attached to, and present for duty with, a unit in the action for which a Distinguished Unit Citation is awarded may wear the Distinguished Unit Citation Emblem as a permanent part of his uniform. An individual who was subsequently assigned or was permanently attached to such a unit but was not present with that unit when its award was won may wear the Distinguished Unit Citation Emblem as a temporary part of his uniform, but only so long as he remains with the unit.

The *Distinguished Unit Citation Emblem* is a dark blue ribbon, 1⅜ inches wide and ⅜ of an inch high, set in a decorative metal frame simulating a laurel wreath (see color plate II, no. 12).

For each subsequent Distinguished Unit Citation, the individual is authorized to wear on the ribbon a bronze oak-leaf cluster—a twig of four oak leaves, 5⁄16 of an inch in length, with three acorns on the stem. The same cluster in silver is authorized for wear in lieu of five bronze oak-leaf clusters.

PRESIDENTIAL UNIT CITATION

Navy

This citation, authorized by Executive Order 9050 on February 6, 1942, as amended on June 28, 1943, is given by the Secretary of the Navy, in the name of the President, to any ship, aircraft, or naval unit, or any Marine Corps aircraft, detachment, or higher unit for outstanding performance in action against an enemy of the United States on or after December 6, 1941. Such service must be comparable to that for which a Navy Cross is awarded to an individual.

An Executive Order of January 10, 1957, provides that the Presidential Unit Citation may also be issued to units of the armed forces of cobelligerent nations serving with United States forces, for outstanding performance in action on or after December 7, 1941, provided that such units meet the standards established for the armed forces of the United States.

When a ship, aircraft, tank unit, or other such unit is awarded the Presidential Unit Citation, it is authorized to display a bronze plaque with the Unit Citation insignia centered in the upper part and the citation engraved below. A company, battalion, regiment, or other such unit awarded the Unit Citation may display a battle streamer with the citation engraved upon the standard.

When a ship that has been cited is lost, its namesake may be authorized to display the plaque, with a notation of when and where the ship was lost; in the event that no new ship is named for the one cited and lost, the plaque may be sent to the United States Naval Academy for display.

All personnel of the cited ship or unit who were actually present at and participated in the action upon which the citation was based shall wear the Citation Ribbon with bronze star permanently. (Blue enamel stars were originally authorized, but these were discontinued early in World War II.) Personnel attached to a cited unit or ship who were not present at or who did not participate in the basic action or actions for which the citation was awarded, or personnel who joined the cited unit after that action,

45

shall wear the Citation Ribbon without star, when attached to that unit.

The *Presidential Unit Citation Ribbon* is regulation size, and consists of three horizontal stripes of equal width in the colors of the Navy and the Marine Corps: from top to bottom, navy blue, gold, and scarlet (see color plate II, no. 13). A star is authorized for each subsequent award of the Presidential Unit Citation.

UNIT COMMENDATION

Navy

This award, established by the Secretary of the Navy on December 18, 1944, with the approval of the President, is conferred on any ship, aircraft, detachment, or other unit in the naval service of the United States which, subsequent to December 6, 1941, shall have distinguished itself by outstanding heroism in action against the enemy, but not of a degree sufficient to justify the award of the Presidential Unit Citation (page 45). It is also awarded to any unit which distinguishes itself by extremely meritorius service not involving combat but in support of military operations, and of such nature as to render the unit outstanding compared to similar units rendering similar service. The service rendered must be comparable to that which would merit the award of a Silver Star Medal or Legion of Merit to an individual.

The *Navy Unit Commendation Ribbon* has a broad wintergreen stripe in the center, flanked on either side by a narrow red stripe, a yellow stripe, and, at the edge, a blue stripe (see color plate II, no. 14). All personnel attached to a unit and actually present and serving therein during the service or occasion for which that unit is commended are authorized to wear the ribbon permanently; a bronze star is worn on the ribbon for each additional such commendation.

OUTSTANDING UNIT AWARD

Air Force

The Department of the Air Force in 1954 authorized this award to be given to units, normally not larger than a wing, which have distinguished themselves by exceptionally meritorious achievement or meritorious service in support of military operations (it is not essential that heroism be involved), or by exceptionally meritorious achievement or service of great national or international significance not involving combat operations against an enemy. In all instances the achievement or service must be above and apart from that of similar units. The Air Force Outstanding Unit Award will not be made to a unit for the same period of service for which a Distinguished Unit Citation (page 44) has been awarded.

Persons assigned or temporarily attached to a unit, and present for duty during the period for which the unit was cited and granted the award, are permanently awarded the *Air Force Outstanding Unit Award Ribbon*. This is of regulation dimensions, with a narrow red stripe in the center, flanked on either side by a narrow white stripe, a broad dark blue stripe, a narrow white stripe, and, at the edge, a narrow red stripe (see color plate II, no. 15). Persons later assigned or attached to a unit so cited may wear the emblem, but only for the period of such assignment or attachment.

Length of Service Awards

GOOD CONDUCT MEDAL

Army

The Army Good Conduct Medal was authorized by Executive Order 8809, on June 28, 1941, for award to enlisted men who shall have honorably completed three continuous years of active military service subsequent to August 26, 1940, and who are recommended by their commanding officers for exemplary behavior, efficiency, and fidelity. Persons awarded this medal must have had character and efficiency ratings of excellent or higher throughout the qualifying period, including time spent in attendance at service schools, and there must have been no convictions by court martial.

During wartime the Good Conduct Medal may be awarded on completion of one year of continuous service rather than three; an executive order of 1943 lowered the qualifying period for World War II, and in 1953 another such order made the one-year ruling apply to service during the Korean conflict (1950-1954), and during any future period in which the United States is at war.

The medal, designed by Joseph Kiselewski, has on the obverse an eagle with wings displayed and inverted, standing on a closed book and a Roman sword. Encircling it is the inscription "Efficiency, Honor, Fidelity." The reverse has a five-pointed star, slightly above center, with a scroll beneath for the recipient's name. Above the star are the words "For Good" and below the scroll the word "Conduct." A wreath, formed of a laurel branch on the left and an oak branch on the right, surrounds the whole design.

The ribbon, designed by Arthur E. DuBois, is of scarlet moiré with three narrow white stripes at either edge.

Only one Good Conduct Medal may be awarded to any individual. For a second or subsequent award, a clasp is worn, consisting of a bar 1⅜ inches long and ⅛ inch wide, which has suspension loops.

Navy

Good Conduct Badge, First Type: 1869–1884

The Navy's award for good conduct, originally known as the Good Conduct Badge, was established by the Secretary of the Navy on April 26, 1869, for award to any man holding a Continuous Service Certificate who had distinguished himself for obedience, sobriety, and cleanliness, and who was proficient in seamanship and gunnery, upon the expiration of his enlistment. Any qualified person receiving three such badges under consecutive re-enlistments (i.e., who re-enlisted within ninety days of his previous discharge) was given the rating of petty officer, which he held during subsequent re-enlistments; he could not be reduced to a lower rating except by the sentence of a court martial.

The badge is a Maltese cross of nickel, 31 mm. in diameter, with a circular medallion bordered in rope bearing the inscription "Fidelity Zeal Obedience," with the initials "U.S.N." in the center. The outer edges of the cross have a rope design. The reverse of the badge is plain. It hangs from a plain open clasp, through which passes a half-inch-wide ribbon of equal stripes of red, white, and blue.

Good Conduct Medal: 1884–Present

A Navy Department General Order of November 21, 1884, authorized a new form of the Good Conduct Badge; the name was subsequently changed to Good Conduct Medal by a directive of April 26, 1896. The award is given to enlisted personnel for three years of continuous active service considered above average in conduct and proficiency. The person recommended must have no sick misconduct, no convictions by court martial, and not more than one nonjudicial punishment in the given three-year period.

The change in design from the style pictured above was made at the suggestion of Commodore Winfield Scott Schley (of Span-

ish-American War fame), Chief of the Navy's Bureau of Equipment and Recruiting. The new design was very similar to that of the badge of the Naval Veterans of the Civil War Association.

The obverse has in its center a full-rigged ship, sailing to the right, with the name *"Constitution"* below it. The medallion is encircled by a rope, knotted at the bottom, and rests upon an anchor, the stock of which appears above and the flukes below. An anchor chain forms a circle around the outer edge of the medal, with the words "United States" between it and the medallion, and the word "Navy" on the central part of the anchor. The reverse has the inscription "Fidelity Zeal Obedience" in raised letters around its outer edge, with a blank center area for the recipient's name and other particulars of the award. The early form of the medal hung from a straight bar clasp; today it is suspended from the conventional ring. The ribbon was originally bright red, but has now been changed to a dark magenta.

A second or subsequent award of the Good Conduct Medal was at one time indicated by a plain clasp with rounded ends. A rope design around the edge had engraved upon it the name of the vessel, with the Continuous Service Certificate number on the reverse. These clasps have been discontinued, and a star is now authorized for each subsequent award of the medal.

Marine Corps

The Marine Corps Good Conduct Medal was authorized on July 20, 1896, by Special Order 49 of the Secretary of the Navy, amended many times since; current changes became effective on July 9, 1953. It is awarded to enlisted men of the Marine Corps, either regular or Reserve, for obedience, sobriety, military efficiency, neatness, bearing, and intelligence, during three years' continuous active service, if they have had no convictions by court martial and not more than one nonjudicial punishment.

Marine Corps veterans of World War I were eligible for the Good Conduct Medal if they had enlisted for the duration of the war but were discharged due to medical disabilities incurred in the line of duty. Men or women of the Marine Corps Reserve assigned to active service during the period from April 6, 1917, to November 11, 1918, were also eligible.

The medal, designed by Major General Charles Heywood, U.S.M.C., ninth Commandant of the Marine Corps (1891-1903), has a gunner standing behind a naval gun of the period in the center of the obverse. This scene is encircled by a rope, with a scroll below it bearing the inscription *"Semper Fidelis."* The medallion is superimposed on an achor, the stock of which appears above, slightly to the left, and the flukes below, slightly to the right. A chain joined to the anchor at the top forms a circle around the edge of the medal, with the inscription "United States Marine Corps" between it and the rope. The reverse of the medal bears the raised legend "Fidelity Zeal Obedience" about a blank area for the recipient's name.

The ribbon attachment is rather unusual in that the medal is attached by a ring to a clasp in the form of a rifle, pointing to the right, which is in turn joined to the ribbon. The ribbon is suspended from a rounded bar with a rope edge, inscribed "U.S. Marine Corps." The scarlet ribbon has a navy blue center stripe.

A second or subsequent award of the Good Conduct Medal was at one time indicated by a bar similar to the ribbon-suspension bar, with a blank center in which was engraved the enlistment period for which the bar was awarded. These bars have been discontinued, and a star is now authorized to indicate each subsequent award.

Coast Guard

The Coast Guard Good Conduct Medal, authorized for issuance on December 12, 1923, is awarded to enlisted personnel of the Coast Guard and the Coast Guard Reserve for periods of service above the average. The medal was originally given for four years' continuous service during the period from May 17, 1920, to June 30, 1934. It is now awarded for three years' continuous service; temporary service is not applicable.

The obverse of the medal shows a small ship (a cutter) within a circle of rope crossed at the bottom, surrounded by the motto of the Coast Guard, *"Semper Paratus."* Around the outer edge of the medal is a chain, with crossed oars at the bottom. The reverse is inscribed "Fidelity Zeal Obedience" around the edge, with a blank area at the center, within a circle of rope, for the recipient's name.

The medal is joined to the ribbon by a straight suspension clasp, and the ribbon is in turn suspended from a straight clasp inscribed "U.S. Coast Guard." The ribbon is maroon with a narrow white center stripe.

A second or subsequent award of the Good Conduct Medal is indicated by a rope-bordered clasp known as the Good Conduct Bar, upon which is engraved the name of the ship that the recipient served on.

Air Force

The Air Force Good Conduct Medal is the same as that of the Army. The ribbon, however, is different; it is sky blue, with three narrow stripes of red, white, and dark blue near each edge.

ARMED FORCES RESERVE MEDAL

Authorized by Executive Order 10163 of September 25, 1950, as amended by Executive Order 10439 of March 19, 1952, the Armed Forces Reserve Medal is awarded to any individual who completes ten years' honorable satisfactory service in any of the reserve components of the United States armed forces, including the National Guard, provided such service is within a period of twelve consecutive years. Prior to July 1, 1949, "satisfactory service" was defined as honorable service in any of these units. Since that date, a member of such a unit must be credited with a minimum of fifty reserve retirement points per anniversary year in order to have that year apply as satisfactory service toward the award of the Armed Forces Reserve Medal.

The medal was designed by the Heraldic Branch of the Army's Quartermaster Corps. Its obverse, which depicts a flaming torch centered upon a crossed powder horn and a bugle, within a design of thirteen stars and thirteen rays, is the same for all services. The reverse of the medal bears the circular inscription "Armed Forces Reserve" about a center which has a different emblem for each of the services:

Army: A Minute Man facing left, with thirteen stars in a circle behind the figure.

Navy: A large sailing ship, seen from the side, under full sail. In front of the ship is an anchor, flukes down, with an eagle, wings spread, superimposed on it.

Marine Corps: The Marine Corps emblem—the globe, an eagle, and an anchor.

Coast Guard: The Coast Guard emblem—crossed anchors with a circular plaque upon them bearing the shield of the Coast Guard.

Air Force: The Air Force emblem—an eagle, wings spread, before a circle with clouds.

National Guard: The National Guard emblem—an eagle with wings spread, crossed fasces in front of it.

The ribbon, which is the same for all the services, has a narrow light blue center stripe, flanked with a wide buff stripe on either side, and alternating narrow stripes of blue and buff —three of blue and two of buff—at either edge.

NAVAL RESERVE MEDAL

1938–1958

This medal, authorized by the Secretary of the Navy on September 12, 1938, was formerly awarded by the Chief of Naval Personnel to officers and enlisted men of the Naval Reserve who had completed ten years' satisfactory federal service in the Naval Reserve Force, National Naval Volunteers, or federally recognized naval militia in active or inactive duty status. A bronze star was authorized for each additional ten years of qualifying service if the individual so requested.

Members of the Naval Reserve were not eligible for this award during a time of war or national emergency until they reported for active duty. After June 30, 1950, a Naval Reservist was required to receive during each anniversary year a total of fifty retirement points to be eligible for the medal.

After the establishment in 1950 of the Armed Forces Reserve Medal, a member of the Naval Reserve who was eligible for the Naval Reserve Medal and also for the Armed Forces Reserve Medal could elect which of the two awards he was to receive. The authorization for awarding the Naval Reserve Medal was terminated on September 12, 1958, and now only the Armed Forces Reserve Medal is given.

The obverse of the Naval Reserve Medal shows an eagle in an attitude of defiance, facing left, with wings raised. The eagle is perched on an anchor, flukes down to the left, and this in turn rests on rocks. In the background are rays and to the left clouds. The reverse of the medal is flat, with the inscription "United States Naval Reserve" encircling the outer edge. At the bottom is a large star and the words "Faithful Service" centered in two lines. The ribbon is bright red, with a narrow stripe of yellow, one of navy blue, and another of yellow at either edge.

ORGANIZED MARINE CORPS RESERVE MEDAL

A directive of the Secretary of the Navy of February 19, 1939, authorized this medal, to be awarded to any officer or enlisted man of the Marine Corps Reserve who subsequent to July 1, 1925, shall have served with an organized unit of the reserve (originally only service in the Fleet Marine Corps Reserve was recognized); have attended four annual field training periods of not less than fourteen days each; and have attended at least thirty-eight drills a year for four consecutive years. Appropriate or equivalent duty or instruction may be credited in lieu of drills. An officer must have received no unsatisfactory fitness reports, and an enlisted man must have attained, upon discharge, an average service record of excellent or above to be eligible.

The obverse, designed by John R. Sinnock, shows two figures walking, the one in the foreground in pre–World War II Marine Corps uniform and the other—his shadow, symbolizing the dual role of the Marine Corps Reservist—in civilian dress. Above the figures is the circular inscription "Marine Corps Reserve" and below them the words "For Service." The reverse is the same as that of the Marine Corps Good Conduct Medal (page 51) designed by Major General Charles Heywood, U.S.M.C.

The first design approved for this medal had the inscription "Fleet Marine Corps Reserve" on the obverse. A small supply of this medal was struck, but it was later decided not to restrict the award to the Fleet Marine Corps Reserve, and a new medal was issued omitting the word "Fleet."

The ribbon has a red center stripe, flanked on either side by a wide yellow stripe, with a narrow blue, a white, and a red stripe at either edge.

MARINE CORPS RESERVE RIBBON

This ribbon, authorized by the Secretary of the Navy on December 17, 1945, is awarded to any member of the Marine Corps Reserve who shall have completed ten years' honorable service in any class or combination of classes of the Marine Corps Reserve, and whose subsequent service, if any, is satisfactory. Service by which a reservist qualifies for either the Armed Forces Reserve Medal or Organized Marine Corps Reserve Medal may not be counted in completing the ten years required for the Marine Corps Reserve Ribbon, and any person who was a member of the Marine Corps Reserve during a time of war and who did not serve on active duty during the course of the war shall not be eligible for this award.

A member of the Marine Corps Reserve who is eligible for the Marine Corps Reserve Ribbon and also for the Armed Forces Reserve Medal may elect which of these awards he will receive. The Marine Corps Reserve Ribbon will not awarded after December 17, 1965; the Armed Forces Reserve Medal will be given for any ten-year qualification period that expires after that date.

The Marine Corps Reserve Ribbon is of regulation size, and features the colors of the Marine Corps, being of gold with a narrow scarlet stripe at either edge (see color plate II, no. 39).

AIR FORCE LONGEVITY SERVICE AWARD RIBBON

The first award to be authorized and designed especially for personnel of the Air Force after it became a separate branch of the armed services, in 1947, was the Air Force Longevity Service Award Ribbon, established by the Department of the Air Force on November 25, 1957. It is awarded to all members of the Air Force on active duty, to reserve components not on active duty, and to all retired personnel on the Air Force retired lists, for an aggregate of four years' honorable service with any branch of the United States armed forces.

The ribbon is of the usual dimensions, and has a broad ultramarine center stripe, with equal stripes of turquoise blue, ultramarine, turquoise, and ultramarine on either side (see color plate II, no. 40). A bronze oak-leaf cluster is worn on the ribbon in lieu of subsequent awards for each additional four years of honorable active federal military service. A silver oak-leaf cluster is worn in lieu of five bronze clusters.

The Air Force Longevity Service Award Ribbon replaces the Federal Service Stripes previously worn by Air Force enlisted personnel.

Training Awards

AMERICAN SPIRIT HONOR MEDAL

This unusual award, authorized by the Secretary of Defense in a directive of Janury 27, 1950, is given to any person who while undergoing a course of basic training in the United States armed forces demonstrates outstanding qualities of leadership, best expressing, in the words of the citation, "the American Spirit—honor, initiative, loyalty and high example to comrades in arms." Recipients of this award, selected by a board of not less than three officers appointed by the commanding officer of a training area, must be serving their first term of enlistment or induction.

The obverse of the medal—which is actually a pocket piece—has a symbolic sunburst, with an American eagle rampant superimposed on it. Within a circle in the sunburst are the words "Serve with Heart, Head and Hand," the motto of the Citizens Committee of the Army and Navy, Inc., a New York organization which is the donor of the medal. Around the perimeter are the words "American Spirit Honor Medal." The reverse shows a hand holding high a lighted torch, with the inscription, slightly above the center, "For High Example to Comrades in Arms."

BAILEY MEDAL

This medal, now discontinued, was authorized by the Navy Department on December 1, 1885, to be awarded annually to one naval apprentice with an outstanding record, in memory of Admiral Theodorus Bailey (1805-1877).

The obverse of the gold medal bears the head of the Admiral, facing right, surrounded by the inscription "Endowed in Memoriam Theodorus Bailey, Obit. 1877," within a wreath. The reverse has the inscription "Conferred on" above a space for the recipient's name, with the words "For Merit in" above another space for the duties specified, and "By Trustees" below.

The ribbon suspender resembles a block and tackle, with a

cable passing around the medal and through the block, which is joined to a ring at the top through which the ribbon passes. The ribbon, much narrower than the regulation width, is cornflower blue. The straight gold bar from which it hangs has a space for an engraved inscription.

PART TWO
SERVICE MEDALS

REVOLUTIONARY WAR
1775-1783

Despite the extraordinary heroism with which the first American soldiers helped to create our nation, there was little official recognition of their services in the form of awards. In 1776, the year after the Continental Congress appointed George Washington as Commander of the American Continental Army, the Congress voted a gold medal for Washington in appreciation of his driving the British out of Boston. That was the young nation's first medal. The Congress gave medals to other commanding officers and admirals during the war, but it did not offer any general award for enlisted men. In the complex process of establishing our new government, the leaders of the country made no provision for honoring the sacrifices which bought the nation's freedom at such places as Ticonderoga, Bunker Hill, Trenton, Valley Forge, Yorktown. To remedy this situation, General Washington, on August 7, 1782, established the Badge of Military Merit. Even this award had a short and limited history, but it was the forerunner of one of our most famous medals.

Badge of Military Merit

This badge, acknowledging "singularly meritorious action," is known to have been awarded to three persons: Sgt. Elijah Churchill, 2nd Regiment, Light Dragoons; Sgt. William Brown, 5th Connecticut Regiment; and Sgt. Daniel Bissell, 2nd Connecticut Regiment. The decoration, though intended to be permanent, then fell into disuse. The award given to Sergeant Churchill is a heart-shaped purple cloth embroidered with a wreath surrounding the word "Merit," and with edges of silver rope. The other extant award is plain purple cloth with silver edging. The badge served as an inspiration for the Legion of Merit and the Medal for Merit, and its design, by Pierre Charles L'Enfant, is the basis for the modern Purple Heart.

"André Medals"

In 1780, Congress created awards for three enlisted men, to be worn as decorations. These "André medals" were given to the three American militiamen (John Paulding, Isaac Van Wart, and David Williams) who captured the British Intelligence officer Major John André. The medal is a rather large oval. The obverse has the word *"Amor"* at the top and the words *"Patriae Vincit"* below, with a flowering plant at both sides joined at the bottom by a bow. In the center is an ornate engraving around the initials of the recipient. The border is beaded and at the top is a beaded loop. The reverse has a laurel branch at the left and a flowering plant at the right, joined at the bottom by a knot. In the center is a decorative shield, under a scroll bearing the word "Fidelity." The top loop and border are beaded.

CIVIL WAR
1861-1865

When Americans fired on Americans at Fort Sumter on April 12, 1861, there began a war that few men on either side believed would be very long or costly. Eleven Southern states, with about nine million people, were fighting twenty-three states of the North (soon to be joined by two more), with about twenty-two million. The North was wakened from its dream of a short, victorious war at the battle of Bull Run (Manassas) on July 21, 1861, when a Confederate force under General Pierre Beauregard routed Union troops under Major General Irvin McDowell. Two years later, at the battle of Gettysburg (July 1-3, 1863), when General Robert E. Lee's attempt to invade the North a second time was defeated by General George G. Meade's Army of the Potomac, the South experienced a defeat which formed the turning point of the war; however, nearly two more years of bloodshed passed before Lee surrendered to General Ulysses S. Grant at Appomattox on April 9, 1865. The victory, which had cost thousands of lives, was darkened further by the assassination of President Lincoln on April 14. But slavery had been abolished and the Union restored.

Several medals and decorations came into existence during the Civil War. Though only the Medal of Honor and special medals authorized by Congress were conferred officially, the following state and Army awards are interesting.

Kearny Medals

Major General Philip Kearny, commander of the Third Division, Army of the Potomac, was killed at the battle of Chantilly on September 1, 1862. On November 29, his officers adopted a resolution that a medal was to be presented to officers who served under Kearny and to enlisted men promoted to commissioned officers' rank before January 1, 1863.

The medal, made by the firm of Ball, Black and Company, is a cross pattée in gold. In the center a circular medallion of black enamel bears the word "Kearny" with a line above and below. Around this is an enameled black band with the inscription in gold, *"Dulce et decorum est pro patria mori."* On the reverse is engraved the number of the cross and the name and rank of the recipient.

The medal is attached to a narrow gold bar suspended from a red ribbon.

On March 13, 1863, General David B. Birney, who had succeeded to Kearny's command, ordered a similar cross in bronze for noncommissioned officers and privates who distinguished themselves in battle. On the obverse of this bronze cross pattée is a ribbon bearing the words "Kearny Cross." On the reverse is centered in one line "Birney's Division," and at the bottom in small letters "Jacobus, Phila.," indicating the designer and die cutter, Peter Jacobus.

The cross is attached to an oblong clasp of fasces and suspended from a red ribbon which hangs from a similar clasp pin.

The Gilmore Medal

On October 28, 1863, Major General Quincy A. Gilmore, commanding the Department of the South, ordered this medal to commemorate the operations before Charleston. The designer is unknown. The obverse shows a fortress surrounded by water. Above this is the legend "Fort Sumter," and below is the date "Aug. 23d 1862." The whole is encircled by thirteen stars. The reverse has the inscription "For Gallant and Meritorious Conduct" around the edge, and at the bottom are three stars. In the center are the words "Presented by" and a facsimile of the General's signature, "Q. A. Gilmore, Maj. Genl." The medal is suspended from a clasp, on which the recipient's name is engraved.

The Army of the James Medal

On October 11, 1864, Major General Benjamin F. Butler, commanding the Army of the James, announced a special medal to honor certain Negro troops in his command for gallantry during the battle of New Market Heights on September 29, 1864.

The obverse of this silver medal shows a bastion being charged by two Negro soldiers. Across the top, a wreath bears the inscription *"Ferro Iis Libertas Perveniet,"* and at the bottom, "U.S. Colored Troops." The reverse has an oak wreath surrounding the inscription "Campaign Before Richmond 1864" in four lines. The whole is encircled by the words "Distinguished for Courage" and two stars. The recipient's name, company, and regiment are engraved on the rim. The designer was Anthony C. Paquet.

The medal is attached to the red, white, and blue ribbon by an ornate suspension. In its center an eagle's claw grasps a sphere to which a ring is attached which passes through the medal. At the top of the ribbon a large oak-leaf pin bears the inscription "Army of the James." The ribbon passes through the back of this pin.

Civil War Medal—Army

This award was authorized by the War Department in 1907 for military service from April 15, 1861, to April 9, 1865—or, for service in Texas, to August 20, 1866.

The medal was designed by the famous artist, Francis D. Millet. The obverse has a bust of Abraham Lincoln, surrounded by the legend "With Malice toward None with Charity for All." The reverse has the inscription "The Civil War 1861-1865" in three lines, surrounded by a wreath formed by a branch of oak on the left and one of olive on the right, joined at the bottom by a knot.

The original ribbon had a narrow white stripe in the center, flanked on either side by equal stripes of red, white, and blue. This was changed in 1913 to half blue (on the left) and half gray.

Civil War Medal—Navy and Marine Corps

This medal was established on June 27, 1908, for award to officers and enlisted men of the Navy and Marine Corps who were in the Naval Service during the Civil War, between April 15, 1861, and April 9, 1865.

Designed by Bailey, Banks and Biddle, the medal has on the obverse a striking representation of the battle between the iron-

clads *Monitor* and *Merrimac*, at Hampton Roads, Va., March 9, 1862. The *Monitor* in the right foreground closes with the *Merrimac* at left center. In the background, to the right, are two wooden ships, one sinking. (The fighting ironclads outmoded wooden warships.) Shells are shown hitting the water, and air bursts are shown overhead. Above this, in an arc, is the inscription "The Civil War." Below the scene are the dates "1861-1865." The reverse has an eagle in the center, with wings spread, facing left and resting on an anchor with draped chain. Below this is the inscription "For service." Below that are a branch of oak on the left and a branch of laurel on the right, joined by a knot. At the top, in an arc, is the inscription "United States Navy" or "United States Marine Corps."

The ribbon is half blue (on the left) and half gray.

Medals of the Confederate States

The medals of the Confederacy were the Davis Guard Medal for the defense of Sabine Pass, September 8, 1863, and the New Market Cross of Honor, awarded to the Virginia Military Institute Cadet Battalion for the battle of New Market, May 15, 1864. The Southern Cross of Honor was a semi-official medal presented to veterans of the Confederate Army by the Daughters of the Confederacy. There were also a number of unofficial medals.

INDIAN WARS
1865-1898

Immediately after the Civil War, the United States Army was engaged in a series of small wars with the Red Man that was to last for over thirty years. The Horse Soldiers—as the Indians called them—were in general a hard-bitten breed of men, all but ignored in their own time, although they have since been much glorified in books and movies. Many of these troopers had been fighting each other just a short time before, wearing the Blue or the Grey. The Indian Wars were comprised of twelve distinct campaigns from 1865 to 1891 plus many engagements, up to 1898, that varied from skirmishes to pitched battles. Hardly a three-month period passed without some expedition, yet the Indian Wars went comparatively unnoticed for some time; Congress did not recognize the fighting until March 1890, when it applied to Indian fighters the term "veterans" in the sense of soldiers who had participated in a campaign against an armed enemy of the United States.

Indian Wars Medal

This award was not authorized by Congress until January 11, 1905, and was established by a War Department General Order only in 1907.

The medal, designed by Francis D. Millet, is bronze. On the obverse is a mounted Indian in war bonnet, carrying a spear. Above the horsemen are the words "Indian Wars," and at the bottom is a buffalo skull at the center of a semicircle of arrowheads. The reverse shows an eagle with wings outspread, standing on a trophy composed of a cannon, crossed flags, spears, an Indian shield, a quiver of arrows, a Cuban machete, and a Sulu kris (bolo knife). Below are the words "For Service." The whole is encircled by the words "United States Army" at the top and thirteen stars below.

The ribbon is deep red with black stripes ¼ inch from each side. Originally red with darker red edges, the ribbon was altered in 1917 to distinguish it from that of the French Legion of Honor.

SPANISH-AMERICAN WAR
1898

On February 15, 1898 an explosion shook Havana Harbor, Cuba, and sank the United States battleship *Maine*. Although the cause of the explosion was never indisputably determined, enraged Americans blamed the Spanish government, and the United States declared war on Spain. The conflict lasted until August 12, and in the peace treaty, signed on December 10, Spain gave up its claim to Cuba, Puerto Rico, the Philippines, and Guam.

The war was chiefly naval, with fighting in both the Atlantic and Pacific Oceans; on May 1 the Asiatic Squadron, under the command of Commodore George Dewey, attacked and destroyed the Spanish fleet in Manila Bay, Philippine Islands.

Manila Bay Medal

This "Dewey Medal" was authorized on June 3, 1898, for officers and men of the Navy and Marine Corps who took part in the battle of Manila Bay.

This medal, one of the handsomest ever crafted in the United States, was designed by Daniel Chester French and struck by Tiffany and Company. On the obverse is a bust of Admiral Dewey, with the inscription "The Gift of the People of the United States to the Officers and Men of the Asiatic Squadron under the Command of Commodore George Dewey." The rim is beaded. On the reverse a finely modeled figure of an American sailor, stripped to the waist, sits on a naval gun, holding across his knees the American flag, his left foot on a small panel on which is engraved the name of the ship on which the recipient served. Encircling all are the words "In Memory of the Victory of Manila Bay, May 1st, 1898."

This medal is unique in its suspension from a bar by a link, with the ribbon (blue and gold—colors of the Navy) *behind* the medal. The bar shows an American eagle with wings spread over the sea, a sword hilt on the right, and an olive branch on the left.

Cardenas Medal of Honor

This was the first medal awarded exclusively to members of a ship of the Revenue Cutter Service (now the Coast Guard) for action during the Spanish-American War. On May 11, 1898, in an attempt to cut a cable guarding the Cardenas harbor entrance, three ships of the blockading American fleet came under heavy fire. First Lt. Frank H. Newcomb brought his ship, the *Hudson,* up to the disabled *Winslow* and towed it out of range of enemy guns.

The medal, designed by the United States Mint in Philadelphia, was awarded in gold to Lieutenant Newcomb, in silver to his officers, and in bronze to the men of his command. The obverse shows a draped winged female figure in a winged helmet, a sword in her right hand and a palm branch in her left. In the background the *Hudson* tows the *Winslow.* Below, in the base of the medal, is inscribed "Cardenas, May 11, 1898." The reverse bears  a nude male figure inscribing with chisel and mallet the words "Joint Resolution of Congress approved May 3, 1900, in Recognition of the Gallantry of the Officers and Men of the Hudson, Who in the Face of Galling Fire Towed the Winslow out of Range of the Enemy's Guns." Below is a wreath in which the recipient's name may be engraved; to the left of the figure is an oak wreath with a palm branch through it.

This interesting but little-known medal, 3⅛ inches in diameter, was not meant to be worn; therefore a companion piece of the usual size was struck. Its ribbon has three equal stripes of Navy blue, yellow, Navy blue; at the top is a suspension bar bearing the name "Cardenas."

The Meritorious Service Medal

The attempt of the crew of the U.S.S. *Merrimac* to block Commander Cervera's fleet in Santiago Harbor in July 1898 was an extraordinary act of heroism. This medal, sometimes called the "Specially Meritorious Medal," was authorized by Congress in March 1901 for award to ninety-three officers and men of the Navy and Marine Corps—the crew of the *Merrimac,* the Naval officers who reconnoitered Santiago from the land side to ascertain the whereabouts of Cervera's fleet, the ships' crews which cut cables under fire, and boat crews who saved the lives of sailors from the sinking Spanish ships at the battle of Santiago; however, it was known to have been actually awarded only to the latter. Although this award is considered a decoration, its place is with the medals of the Spanish-American War, as it was not awarded at any other time. Since so few were awarded, the medal, of course, is very rare.

The medal is a bronze cross pattée with a medallion in the center, bearing an anchor in a wreath of oak and laurel, surrounded by the inscription "U.S. Naval Campaign, West Indies." The arms are inscribed "Specially Meritorious Service 1898." On the reverse are placed the name and rank of the recipient and the event and date for which it was awarded. The designer of the medal is unknown.

The ribbon is scarlet.

West Indies Naval Campaign Medal, 1898

This medal, popularly known as the "Sampson Medal," was authorized on March 3, 1901, for members of the Navy and Marine Corps who took part in West Indies naval operations from April 27 to August 14, 1898.

The obverse, designed by Charles E. Barber, shows a bust of Admiral Sampson. In a semicircle above are the words "U.S. Naval Campaign, West Indies, 1898." At the left are the words "William T. Sampson" and at the right, "Commander in Chief." The reverse, designed by George T. Morgan, shows a group on a ship's deck. In the center an officer directs fire; at the left is a sailor with a rapid-fire gun, and at the right a Marine with a rifle. Below is specified the engagement with date of the campaign for which the medal was issued. At the top of the ribbon is a brooch pin with the name of the recipient's ship. Additional engagement bars were authorized; they have a rope border around the name of the battle, with a small anchor at each end. The medal was issued for forty-seven engagements or skirmishes. Some were awarded with six or seven engagement bars.

The moiré ribbon is of three equal stripes—red, blue, red.

73 ✠

Marines who landed in Cuba as a fighting expeditionary unit were awarded this medal with a blank bar at the top, no name of the ship showing.

West Indies Campaign Medal

This award was authorized in 1908 for members of the Navy and Marine Corps who served aboard ships in the West Indies. It was rarely given, as most of those men were entitled to the "Sampson Medal" and two awards could not be given for the same service. For this reason it was later discontinued.

The design, by Bailey, Banks and Biddle, is almost the same as that of the Navy Spanish Campaign Medal. It shows Morro Castle, which guards Havana Harbor, with a stack of cannon balls in the foreground. Above is the legend "West Indies Campaign," and below is "1898." The reverse, except for the inscriptions, corresponds to that of the Navy and Marine Corps Civil War Medal (page 68).

The ribbon was originally the same as that of the first Spanish Campaign Medal for the Navy—yellow with a red stripe ⅛ inch from either side. This was changed in 1913 to blue, yellow, blue, with narrow yellow edges.

Spanish Campaign Medal—Army

This award was authorized in January 1905 for Army service in 1898 in Cuba, May 11 to July 17; in Puerto Rico, July 24 to August 13; and the Philippine Islands, July 24 to August 13.

The medal, designed by Francis D. Millet, has on the obverse a castle within a circle composed of the words "War with Spain" on the top and "1898" below, with a branch of tobacco plant and a stalk of sugar cane at the left and right of the date. The reverse is the same as that of the Indian Wars Medal.

The ribbon was originally red, blue, yellow—the colors of the Spanish flag. In 1913, however, in deference to a then friendly nation, the colors were changed to yellow and blue.

Spanish Campaign Medal—
Navy and Marine Corps

The Navy in 1908 authorized a medal for all officers and men of the Navy and Marine Corps for service afloat in the theater of active naval operations, or on shore in Cuba, Puerto Rico, the Philippines, or Guam between May and August 16, 1898.

The medal, designed by Bailey, Banks and Biddle, is bronze. On the obverse is a view of Morro Castle, with the legend "Spanish Campaign" above and "1898" below. The reverse is the same as that of the Navy Civil War Medal.

The ribbon was originally yellow with two red stripes near each edge—the colors of the Spanish Navy. This was changed to the present colors—yellow and blue—for the same reason the Army ribbon colors were changed in 1913.

Spanish War Service Medal

This medal, sometimes called the "National Guard Medal," was authorized on July 9, 1918, for persons who served between April 20, 1898, and April 11, 1899, but were not eligible for the Spanish Campaign Medal.

The obverse, designed by Colonel J. R. M. Taylor, U.S. Army, shows a sheathed Roman sword lying on a tablet inscribed "For Service in the Spanish War" and surrounded by a wreath. The reverse, designed by Bailey, Banks and Biddle, has the United States coat of arms with a scroll below, all surrounded by a wreath displaying the Infantry, Artillery, and Cavalry insignia.

The ribbon is emerald green with two yellow stripes.

Army of Puerto Rico Occupation Medal

This was authorized in 1919 for service in Puerto Rico, August 14 to December 10, 1898.

The obverse, designed by the Army Heraldic Section, resembles that of the Spanish Campaign Medal. It has a similar castle with the words "Army of Occupation Porto Rico" along the upper edge, and "1898" at the bottom, with a stalk of sugar cane at the right and a tobacco-plant branch at the left. The reverse is the same as that of the Indian Wars Medal.

The ribbon has a red stripe in the center flanked by narrow yellow stripes, wide dark blue stripes, and narrow red stripes.

Army of Cuba Occupation Medal

This medal was established in 1915 for service in Cuba, July 18, 1898, to May 20, 1902.

The obverse, designed by the Army Heraldic Section, shows the Cuban Republic coat of arms resting on a fasces and flanked by sprays of oak and laurel. Above it are the dates "1898 1902." Around the circumference are the words "Army of Occupation, Military Government of Cuba." The reverse is the same as that of the Indian Wars Medal.

The ribbon has a blue band in the center, flanked stripes of yellow, red, and blue.

THE PHILIPPINE INSURRECTION
1899-1913

On February 4, 1899, Philippine patriots launched an assault against United States occupation troops in Manila. The Americans then embarked on a costly war against the guerrillas, which lasted officially until July 4, 1902, when the military government was superseded by a civil one. Hostilities, however, continued in some places until 1913.

Philippine Campaign Medal—Army

Authorized in 1905, this medal was awarded for service in the Philippines during the insurrection. It was also extended to cover actions in various parts of the islands through 1913.

The medal was designed by Francis D. Millet. On the obverse is a coconut palm tree with a Roman lamp at one side, symbolizing the enlightenment of the islands under American rule. On the other side are the scales of justice. Around the scene is a circle composed of the words "Philippine Insurrection 1899." The reverse is the same as that of the Indian Wars Medal.

The ribbon is blue flanked by broad stripes of red and narrow blue borders.

Philippine Campaign Medal—
Navy and Marine Corps

This medal was authorized in 1908 for Navy and Marine Corps officers and men who served in sixty-four ships in Philippine waters at various specified periods between February 1899 and November 1905, or who served ashore on Mindanao.

The obverse shows an old gate in the city wall of Manila, with the words "Philippine Campaign" along the edge above and "1899-1903" below, flanked by laurel branches. The reverse is the same as that of the Navy Civil War Campaign Medal. The design is by Bailey, Banks and Biddle.

The original Navy ribbon, which had three equal stripes of red, yellow, red, was altered in 1913 to approximate the appearance of the Army ribbon.

Philippine Congressional Medal

This medal was established June 29, 1906, for members of the Army who volunteered to remain beyond their discharge date to help suppress the insurrection, and who were ashore in the Philippines between February 4, 1899, and July 4, 1902.

The medal was designed by Francis D. Millet. On the obverse is shown a color bearer holding a United States flag and supported by two men with rifles on their shoulders. The flag extends to the rim of the medal between the words "Philippine Insurrection"; at the bottom is the date "1899." The reverse has the words "For Patriotism, Fortitude, and Loyalty" in a wreath composed of a branch of pine on the left and one of palm on the right, joined by a knot.

The ribbon is dark blue in the center, flanked by narrow white, red, white, and blue stripes.

THE BOXER REBELLION
1900-1901

In China in 1900, resentment against powerful Western interests exploded in the form of a revolt by the century-old secret society I Ho Ch'üan, "Fists of Righteous Harmony," known to English-speaking people as the "Boxers." The rebellion was crushed in 1901 by the Peking Relief Expedition, an international force made up of troops from Great Britain, France, Italy, Germany, Austria, Russia, Japan, and the United States.

The part played by Americans is indicated in the Roll of Honor; 60 Congressional Medals of Honor were awarded—34 to the Marine Corps, 22 to the Navy, and 4 to the Army.

China Relief Expedition Medal—Army

Authorized in 1905, this medal was awarded for Army service ashore in China with the Peking Relief Expedition between June 20, 1900, and May 27, 1901.

The obverse, designed by Francis D. Millet, shows the Imperial Chinese five-toed dragon within a circle composed of the words "China Relief Expedition" across the top and "1900-1901" at the bottom. The striking representation makes this one of the most unusual American medals. The reverse is the same as that of the Indian Wars Medal.

The ribbon is yellow (the color of the Manchu Dynasty, then on the Chinese throne), with narrow dark blue edges.

China Relief Expedition Medal—
Navy and Marine Corps

This medal was authorized June 27, 1908, for officers and enlisted men of the Navy and Marine Corps who served ashore in China with the Peking Relief Expedition between May 24, 1900, and May 27, 1901. It was also awarded for service on certain vessels in Chinese waters during the same period.

The medal was designed by Bailey, Banks and Biddle. The obverse shows the Chien Men, the main gate to the walled city of Peking, with the Imperial Chinese dragon lying below; around this is a circle bearing the inscription "China Relief Expedition" above and "1900" or "1901" below. The reverse is the same as that of the Navy Civil War Campaign Medal.

The ribbon, originally yellow with narrow black stripes near each edge (the colors of the Manchu government), was changed in 1913 to the Army ribbon, yellow with dark blue edges.

PACIFICATION OF CUBA
1906-1909

Four and a half years after the Spanish American War, United States occupation of Cuba came to an end when a Cuban republic was formed, with Thomas Estrada Palma as the first President. Political, economic, and social difficulties, however, led to insurrection, and President Palma eventually appealed to the United States for intervention. On September 29, 1906, Palma resigned and the United States proclaimed a provisional government. A new government was formed on January 28, 1908, with General José Miguel as President. The last American troops were withdrawn on April 1, 1909.

Cuban Pacification Medal—Army

This medal was authorized in 1909 for officers and men of the Army of Cuban Pacification who served in Cuba between October 6, 1906, and April 1, 1909.

The obverse, designed by the Army Heraldic Section, shows the Cuban coat of arms within a shield in the center, resting on fasces, surmounted by a cap of liberty bearing a single star. Below are branches of oak and laurel. On each side of the shield stands an American soldier in the dress uniform of the period, with a rifle at parade rest. The words "Cuban Pacification" appear above this in two lines and below are the dates "1906-1909." The reverse is the same as that of the Indian Wars Medal.

The ribbon has a wide dark tan center, with narrower stripes of red, white, and blue of equal width on each side.

Cuban Pacification Medal—
Navy and Marine Corps

This medal was authorized on August 13, 1909, for officers and enlisted men of the Navy and Marine Corps who served ashore in

Cuba or upon certain designated ships between September 12, 1906, and April 1, 1909.

The obverse, designed by Bailey, Banks and Biddle, shows the figure of Columbia with a sheathed sword hanging from her belt. In her left hand she holds a flag, and in her right hand an olive branch, which she is offering to a Cuban who is kneeling before her. A tropical scene forms the background, and a dove of peace hovers above the figures. In a circular form at the top of the medal are the words "Cuban Pacification 1908." The reverse is the same as the Civil War Campaign medal for both the Navy and Marine Corps respectively.

The ribbon is the same as that of the Army medal.

NICARAGUAN CAMPAIGN 1912

In 1912 the Nicaraguan government requested United States aid in suppressing a revolution. Because of this urgent request and the imminent danger to American lives and property, an expedition was formed. It consisted of eight ships carrying extra complements of Marines. The first United States troops arrived on July 29, 1912. After numerous small engagements in the jungles the revolutionary forces were defeated and the American troops were withdrawn on November 2, 1912.

Nicaraguan Campaign Medal

This medal was authorized on September 22, 1913, for officers and enlisted men of the Navy and Marine Corps who served ashore or on the eight ships of the expedition between August 28 and November 2, 1912.

The medal was designed by Bailey, Banks and Biddle. On the obverse the Nicaraguan volcano Mount Momotombo, in the center, appears to be rising from Lake Managua, surrounded by a tropical forest. Above this scene in circular form are the words "Nicaraguan Campaign." The date "1912" is centered at the bottom of the medal, with a branch of laurel to the right and a branch of oak to the left. The reverse is the same as that of the Navy and Marine Corps Civil War Medal.

The ribbon is dark crimson wtih a broad navy blue stripe near each edge.

THE MEXICAN WAR
1911-1917

The turmoil following the Mexican Revolution of 1910 led to numerous battle engagements between United States and Mexican forces from 1911 to 1917, when a reform constitution was adopted. The most important of these started on March 9, 1916, when Francisco "Pancho" Villa crossed the border with a band of men and raided Columbus, New Mexico, killing sixteen citizens. On the next day the United States initiated the Punitive Expedition to Mexico, under the command of General John J. Pershing. On June 17, 1916, the Mexican government announced that it would resist any further moves by American troops inside its borders. The American expedition withdrew without having captured Villa.

From January 1, 1916, to April 6, 1917, a large portion of the regular Army and about 150,000 National Guardsmen took part in the expedition or were trained on the Mexican border.

Mexican Service Medal—Army

This medal was authorized in 1917 for members of the Army and the National Guard for service in expeditions or engagements during the period 1911 to 1917, in Mexico and along the border in Texas and Arizona.

The obverse, designed by Colonel J. R. M. Taylor, shows a yucca plant in bloom, with mountains in the background. The words "Mexican Service" form a semicircle at the top, and at the bottom are the dates "1911-1917." The reverse is the same as that of the Indian Wars Medal.

The ribbon has a dark blue stripe in the center, flanked by yellow stripes of equal width, with narrow green stripes on each edge.

Mexican Service Medal—
Navy and Marine Corps

This medal was authorized February 11, 1918, for officers and en-
listed men of the Navy and Marine Corps who served on shore
during the Vera Cruz expedition from April 21 to 23, 1914.
It was also awarded to personnel of certain ships for service from
April 21 to November 26, 1914, and from March 14, 1916, to
February 7, 1917, and to any other Navy and Marine Corps mem-
bers who participated in engagements between United States and
Mexican armed forces.

Designed by Bailey, Banks and Biddle, the medal shows on the
obverse the old castle of San Juan de Ulúa in the Veracruz harbor.
The word "Mexico" appears in a circular border above the scene,
with "1911-1917" below and a cactus branch at each side. The
reverse is the same as that of the Navy and Marine Corps Civil
War medals.

The ribbon is the same as that of the Army medal.

Mexican Border Service Medal

Established on July 9, 1918, this medal was awarded to National
Guard members who served on the Mexican border between May
9, 1916, and March 24, 1917, and to regular Army members who
served with the Border Patrol between January 1, 1916, and
April 6, 1917. It was not awarded, however, to persons eligible
for the Mexican Service Medal. This award is often erroneously
called the "National Guard Medal."

The design, by Colonel J. R. M. Taylor, is the same as that of
the Spanish War Service Medal, except that the inscription on the
obverse is "For Service on the Mexican Border."

The ribbon has a yellow center flanked by green bands of the
same width; the colors are the same as those of the ribbon of the
Spanish War Service Medal.

HAITI SERVICE
1915

After a long period of civil strife in Haiti, American Navy and Marine Corps personnel were sent there at the request of France. Some Marines went into the interior to subdue native Cacos who were terrorizing the people and disrupting transportation and communications. Some order was restored, and a treaty was ratified in 1916, providing for the Marines to stay in Haiti. This occupation lasted until 1934.

Haitian Campaign Medal, 1915

This medal was authorized on June 22, 1917, for award to members of the Navy and Marine Corps who served in Haiti, or were attached to specified ships, between July 9 and December 5, 1915.

The design was by Bailey, Banks and Biddle. The obverse shows a view from the sea of the mountains of Cap Haitien coming down to meet a tropical shoreline; a palm tree stands at the left. Above, in a semicircle, are the words "Haitian Campaign," and below is the date "1915." The reverse is the same as that of the Navy and Marine Corps Civil War Medals. (The medal is shown here with a 1919-1920 bar; see page 91.)

The ribbon is navy blue with two narrow stripes of scarlet at the center. The colors are those of Haiti.

DOMINICAN CAMPAIGN 1916

On May 5, 1916, the fighting between political factions in the Dominican Republic reached a climax. Two companies of United States Marines were landed there to protect the American and Haitian legations, and a force of sailors also was landed to seize Fort San Geronimo, needed as a base of operations. The American forces remained until order was restored and the government solidified, in December 1916.

Dominican Campaign Medal, 1916

Authorized on December 29, 1921, this medal was awarded to members of the Navy and Marine Corps who served in the Dominican Republic, or were attached to specific ships, between May 5 and December 4, 1916.

The medal, designed by A. A. Weinman, shows on the obverse the "Tower of Homage" in the capital city, with sea wall and waves. Below is the date "1916," and above, in a semicircle, the words "Dominican Campaign." The reverse—a new one for the Navy and Marine Corps—shows an eagle perched on an anchor, over sprigs of laurel between the words "For Service." At the top in a semicircle is inscribed "United States Navy" or "United States Marine Corps."

The ribbon is red with two narrow blue stripes at the center. This pattern is the reverse of that for the Haitian Campaign Medal.

WORLD WAR I

The United States declared war on Germany on April 6, 1917, and the first advance American troops landed in France in June. By October, they numbered almost two million men. The first American casualties were three soldiers killed by German raiders near Bathelémont on November 3. American Expeditionary Force divisions began to help tip the scales against the Germans at such places as the Aisne sector (May 27-June 5, 1918), Château-Thierry (May 31-July 9), Montdidier-Noyon (June 9-13), and Belleau Wood (June 6-25). They took part in Marshal Foch's counterattack, spearheading the Aisne-Marne offensive (July 18-August 6) and crushing the St. Mihiel salient (September 12-16). There are thirteen clasps honoring the various battles in which Americans fought; some of the famous specific engagements are included in the general headings listed on the opposite page. The last commemorates the Meuse-Argonne offensive, the final and greatest battle of the war, in which an American Army of over a million men took part. This battle, involving forty-seven days of continual combat, cracked the Hindenburg line, shattered the German Armies, and ended in victory on November 11, 1918.

Victory Medal, World War I

This award was authorized in 1919 for members of the United States armed forces who served on active duty between April 6, 1917, and November 11, 1918; it includes service in Russia.

The medal, designed by James Earle Fraser, shows on the obverse a female winged figure, symbolic of victory. In her left hand is a shield, and in her right a short sword, pointed down. The wings extend to the edge of the medal, and her head is surrounded by a crown of rays. The reverse has a shield in the center representing the coat of arms of the United States, with the letters "U.S." surmounted by a fasces. At the top, in a semicircle, is the inscription "The Great War for Civilization," and on the sides are the names of the Allied nations: on the left, "France, Italy, Serbia,

Japan, Montenegro, Russia, Greece"; on the right, "Great Britain, Belgium, Brazil, Portugal, Rumania, China." At the base, completing the circle, are six stars.

The ribbon has a double rainbow pattern, a dark red center stripe flanked by blending colors: orange, yellow, green, blue, and purple.

Clasps were authorized for wear with this medal, bearing the names of battle, country, or duty station. They are thin bars; battle clasps have a star at each end, and service clasps have no stars. Navy and Marine Corps members, as well as those of the Army, may wear the clasps that are marked in the list below by an asterisk.

The clasps were awarded for the following:

Battle clasps: *Cambrai*, November 20-December 4, 1917. *Somme Offensive*, March 21-April 6, 1918. *Lys*, April 9-27, 1918. *Aisne*, May 27-June 5, 1918. *Montdidier-Noyon*, June 9-15, 1918. *Champagne-Marne*, July 15-18, 1918. *Aisne-Marne*, July 18-August 6, 1918. *Somme Offensive*, August 18-November 11, 1918. *Oise-Aisne*, August 18-November 11, 1918. *Ypres-Lys*, August 19-November 11, 1918. *St. Mihiel*, September 12-16, 1918. *Vittorio-Veneto*, October 24-November 4, 1918. *Meuse-Argonne*, September 20-November 11, 1918.

Service clasps: *England*, April 6, 1917-November 11, 1918. *France*, April 6, 1917-November 11, 1918. *Italy*, April 6, 1917-November 11, 1918. *Russia*, November 12, 1918-August 5 1919. *Siberia*, November 12, 1918-April 1, 1920.

There was also a "Defense Sector" clasp.

The Navy authorized a series of service clasps in addition to those mentioned above. The clasp is rectangular, with a border of rope design. Centered in raised letters on the bar is the service or duty-station name. They are: *Overseas, Armed Guard, Atlantic Fleet, Aviation, Destroyer, Escort, Grand Fleet, Mine Laying, Mine Sweeping, Mobile Base, Naval Battery, Salvage, Subchaser, Submarine, Transport, and West Indies*—all for service in Haiti, Dominican Republic, Cuba, and the Virgin Islands between April 6, 1917, and November 11, 1918; and *White Sea*, for Russia

(November 12, 1918–August 5, 1919), and Siberia (November 12, 1918–April 1, 1920).

A ³⁄₁₆-inch silver star worn on the Victory Medal indicates a citation for gallantry in action. Holders of such stars were awarded the Silver Star Medal on its inception in 1933. The small star also indicated a commendation by the Secretary of the Navy; holders of this award were not entitled to the Silver Star Medal.

A small bronze Maltese cross was awarded to members of the Marine Corps and the Navy Medical Corps who served in France during World War I but did not participate in any engagements.

Army of Occupation of Germany Medal

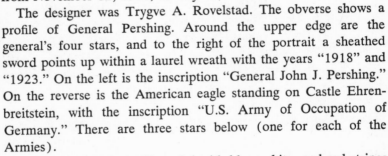

This medal was established on November 21, 1941, for all members of the Army, Navy, Marine Corps, and Coast Guard (or the nearest kin surviving) who served in Germany or Austria-Hungary from November 12, 1918, to July 11, 1923.

The designer was Trygve A. Rovelstad. The obverse shows a profile of General Pershing. Around the upper edge are the general's four stars, and to the right of the portrait a sheathed sword points up within a laurel wreath with the years "1918" and "1923." On the left is the inscription "General John J. Pershing." On the reverse is the American eagle standing on Castle Ehrenbreitstein, with the inscription "U.S. Army of Occupation of Germany." There are three stars below (one for each of the Armies).

The ribbon is black silk moiré with blue, white, and red stripes at either side. The black represents Germany, and the red, white, and blue represent the United States.

HAITIAN CAMPAIGN
1919-1920

In 1915 the *Gendarmerie d'Haiti*, a national police force of Haitians and American Marines under Marine control, had been organized to assume military and police duties throughout the country. Against this Gendarmerie the Caco chief Charlemagne Perlate launched a series of attacks, with his followers and the peasants who had been forced to join them. The Marine Brigade was requested to help suppress the uprising, and carried on an intensive campaign. By the end of June 1920, thousands of outlaws, constituting almost one-fifth of the population of Haiti, had been captured or had surrendered, and the duty of policing the country was gradually shifted back to the Gendarmerie.

Haitian Campaign Medal, 1919-1920

This medal was authorized on December 29, 1921 for officers and enlisted men of the Navy and Marine Corps who participated in the operations in Haiti or were attached to specified vessels serving in Haitian waters, between April 1, 1919, and June 15, 1920.

The medal is the same as the Haitian Campaign medal of 1915 except that the date "1915" is replaced by "1919-1920." Men who had served in Haiti in 1915 and again in 1919-1920 were awarded a clasp to be worn on the ribbon of the 1915 medal, in lieu of the 1919-1920 medal. This clasp has a rope border, with the dates "1919-1920" centered and a star at either edge. It is replaced by a bronze star when the service ribbon alone is worn.

The ribbon is the same as that of the 1915 medal.

There is also a medal in existence that has the date "1919" only. It is believed that this is a very early strike of the 1919-1920 medal.

NICARAGUAN CAMPAIGN 1927

The coup d'état of 1925 in Nicaragua, by which Emiliano Chamorro forced himself into presidential office, led to a dispute over Liberal leader Juan B. Sacasa, who, after fleeing the country, asked Washington to recognize him as President. This the United States refused to do, and when Mexico did grant him recognition the United States moved to end the revolution by isolating the Sacasa forces. United States Marines began landing in Nicaragua in January 1927 for this purpose, and to protect American interests in the country. Most of the fighting—principally isolated engagements—had ended by 1928, but one rebel leader, Augusto Sandino, continued the battle with the government. Under his leadership, attacks occurred periodically until 1933, at which time the last Marine contingent departed.

Second Nicaraguan Campaign Medal

This medal was authorized on November 8, 1929 for members of the Navy and Marine Corps who served on shore in Nicaragua or aboard certain vessels of the Navy serving in Nicaraguan waters, between August 27, 1926, and January 2, 1933; it was also awarded to members of the United States Army who cooperated in operations in this area.

The obverse, designed by Albert Stewart, shows the figure of Columbia, clothed in mail and flowing skirt. With sword in hand, she shields two citizens standing behind her. Behind these figures in the base of the medal are wave scrolls, and below them are the dates "1926-1930." At the top, in circular form, is the inscription "Second Nicaraguan Campaign." The reverse, designed by A. A. Weinman, is the same as that of the Dominican Campaign Medals for the Navy and Marine Corps for their respective services.

The ribbon is scarlet, with eight narrow blue-gray stripes.

CHINA SERVICE
1927-1939

Twenty-four years after the Boxer Rebellion of 1900, a new Chinese nationalist movement began which was bent on driving out foreign business and development. The situatiori became steadily worse, and in 1927 about five thousand United States Marines were sent to Tientsin, Peking, and the International Settlement of Shanghai. Some clashes took place; the only serious one occurred on March 24, 1927, when American and British gunboats, which had been sent to patrol the Yangtze River, fired upon nationalist troops at Nanking to stop them from robbing and killing foreign nationals. In 1930, when another civil war flared up, United States Marine and Navy units were once again sent into the Yangtze area to protect American lives and property. This period of duty was called the Yangtze Service.

In 1937 the 6th Marine Regiment and a battery of anti-aircraft formed the 2nd Brigade in the defense and protection of the International Settlement in Shanghai against the Japanese. Shanghai fell to the Japanese, but the International Settlement remained neutral, under the protection of the Marines. During this period the gunboat U.S.S. *Panay* was bombed and destroyed (December 12, 1937). Though the Marines continued on garrison duty in Shanghai until just before the bombing of Pearl Harbor, the period authorized by the medal extended only to 1939.

Yangtze Service Medal

This award was established on April 28, 1930, for members of the Navy and Marine Corps who served on shore at Shanghai or in the valley of the Yangtze with the landing forces between September 3, 1926, and October 21, 1927, and between March 1, 1930, and December 31, 1932; and to members attached to certain vessels during those periods.

The obverse, designed by John R. Sinnock, shows a Chinese junk with sails at half-mast. Above is the inscription "Yangtze

Service." The reverse is the same as that of the Dominican Campaign Medal for the Navy and Marine Corps.

The ribbon is deep blue, with red and yellow stripes near each side.

China Service Medal

This medal was authorized on August 23, 1940, for Navy and Marine Corps members who participated in the operations in China, or were attached to certain vessels in the China area, between July 7, 1937, and September 7, 1939.

The obverse, designed by George H. Snowden, shows a Chinese junk under full sail, with the words "China" above and "Service" below, in a circular inscription. The reverse is the same as that of the Dominican Campaign Medal for the Navy and Marine Corps.

The deep yellow ribbon has a narrow red stripe near each edge.

China Service Medal (Extended)

Officers and enlisted men of the Armed Forces who participated in operations in China, including Formosa, between September 2, 1945, and April 1, 1957, are authorized to wear the medal; if they are entitled to it for earlier service, they may wear a bronze star on the ribbon.

WORLD WAR II

On December 7, 1941, when the Japanese attacked Pearl Harbor, the United States suddenly became part of the great war which had been going on since Germany invaded Poland on September 1, 1939. On August 6, 1945, the Japanese City of Hiroshima disappeared under a huge mushroom-shaped cloud that signaled a new era; on August 9, a second atomic blast obliterated Nagasaki. The war in Europe had ended on May 8, and now Japan surrendered; the formal capitulation was signed on September 2, 1945. World War II had cost the United States alone four trillion dollars, and had taken forty million lives all over the world.

The enormous scope of the war is reflected in the lists of operations for which campaign medals were awarded. For the Army over twenty areas in the Asiatic-Pacific Theatres are named, ranging from the Philippine Islands (December 7, 1941–May 1942) to the China Offensive (May 5–September 2, 1945); in the European–African–Middle Eastern Theatres there are about twenty, beginning with the Egypt-Libya Campaign (July 11, 1942–February 12, 1943) and including the European Air Offensive (July 4, 1942–June 5, 1944), the Normandy Campaign (June 6–July 24, 1944), and—last—the Po Valley Campaign (April 5–May 8, 1945). The lists of Navy campaigns for the European–African–Middle Eastern Theatres total more than forty and include the North African Occupation (November 8, 1942–July 9, 1943), Salerno landings (September 9–21, 1943), and the Normandy Invasion (June 6–25, 1944) as well as a series of escort, anti-submarine, armed guard, and special operations with such almost-anonymous designations as Convoy ON-166 (February 20-25, 1943) or Task Group 21.12 (April 29–June 20, 1943). The Navy's list of operations honored by the Asiatic–Pacific Campaign Medal numbers over two hundred; the list begins with Pearl Harbor–Midway (December 7, 1941) and extends past the official date of surrender to March 1946, with several mopping-up operations.

American Defense Service Medal

This medal was established on June 28, 1941, for members of the United States armed forces for service during the period that included the limited national emergency proclaimed on September 8, 1939, and the unlimited emergency proclaimed on May 27, 1941; it was later extended to cover the period up to December 7, 1941.

Designed by Lee Lawrie, the medal has on the obverse a female figure representing Liberty, holding a shield and brandishing a sword. She stands on live oak with branches terminating in four leaves, representing the Army, Navy, Marine Corps, and Coast Guard. (The Air Force did not become a separate branch of service until September 18, 1947.) Above this is the inscription "American Defense." The reverse has the inscription "For Service during the Limited Emergency Proclaimed by the President on 8 September 1939 or during the limited emergency proclaimed by the President on 27 May 1941." Below this is a spray of seven leaves.

The ribbon is yellow with narrow red, white, and blue stripes near each edge.

Several clasps were awarded with the medal. The Army had a "Foreign Service" clasp for service outside the continental limits of the United States. The Navy and Marine Corps each had two clasps. The "Fleet" clasp was awarded for service on vessels of the fleet, or of the Naval Transportation Service, or under the command of the Chief of Naval Operations. The "Base" clasp is for service on shore at bases and naval stations outside the continental limits of the United States—this included Alaska and Hawaii at the time. The Coast Guard also authorized a "Sea" clasp, because Coast Guard personnel were at sea at the time, but were not serving as members of fleet units. When the ribbon is worn without the medal, bronze stars are worn in lieu of clasps.

Personnel of the Navy, Marine Corps, and Coast Guard who served on board certain vessels operating in actual combat with the enemy during the specified period in the Atlantic Ocean are entitled to a bronze "A" on the medal ribbon.

American Campaign Medal

This medal was established by Executive Order on November 6, 1942, and amended by another Executive Order on March 15, 1946, which set the closing date.

It is awarded to all members of the armed forces who, between December 7, 1941, and March 2, 1946, served on land or aboard certain ships, for an aggregate period of one year within the continental limits of the United States, or for thirty consecutive days or sixty nonconsecutive days outside the continental limits but within the American Theater of Operations.

Designed by the Heraldic Section of the Army, the medal shows on the obverse a Navy cruiser under full steam with a B-24 bomber overhead and a sinking enemy submarine above three waves. In the background are some buildings representing the arsenal of democracy. Above is the inscription "American Campaign." The reverse shows an American bald eagle facing left, standing defiantly on a rock symbolizing democracy. On the left are the dates "1941-1945," and on the right are the words "United States of America."

The ribbon has four wide stripes of bright azure blue; in the center are three narrow stripes—dark blue, white, and red—and near each side are narrow stripes of white, red, black, white; the red and white represent Japan, and the black and white Germany.

Naval personnel who participated in certain specified operations—escort, anti-submarine armed guard, and others—were awarded one bronze star for each operation, to be worn with this medal.

European-African-Middle Eastern Campaign Medal

This medal was established by Executive Order on November 6, 1942, and amended by another Executive Order on March 15, 1946, which set the closing date. It is awarded to all members of the United States armed forces who served in the prescribed area or aboard certain ships of the Navy between December 7, 1941, and November 8, 1945.

The design is by the Heraldic Section of the Army. The obverse shows an LST in the background with landing craft and troops under fire. An airplane flies overhead, and above the scene are the words "European African Middle Eastern Campaign" in three lines. The reverse is the same as that of the American Theatre Campaign Medal.

In the center of the ribbon are three narrow stripes of red, white, and blue, representing the United States. These are flanked by wider stripes of green, symbolizing the seas, forests, and pastures of Europe. The three narrow stripes at the left are green, white, and red, for Italy; the three at the right are white, black, and white, for Germany. The wider stripes at each edge are brown, for the soil of Africa and Europe.

Asiatic-Pacific Campaign Medal

This medal, established on November 6, 1942, is awarded to all officers and enlisted men of the United States armed forces who, between December 7, 1941, and March 2, 1946, served on active duty in the prescribed area or upon certain ships.

The medal was designed by the Army Heraldic Section. The obverse shows troops landing in a tropical scene, under a palm tree, with a báttleship, aircraft carrier, and submarine in the background and an airplane overhead. At the top of the medal, in a semicircle, is the inscription "Asiatic Pacific Campaign." The reverse is the same as that of the American Campaign Medal.

The ribbon is predominantly bright orange-yellow, representing the tropical Pacific. In the center are narrow stripes of red, white, and blue, symbolizing the United States, and near each side are narrow stripes of white, red, white, symbolizing Japan.

Victory Medal, World War II

This medal was authorized on July 6, 1945, for members of the United States armed forces who served on active duty at any time between December 7, 1941, and December 31, 1946. It was also awarded to members of the Philippine Armed Forces.

The design was by the Army Heraldic Section. The obverse shows a figure of Liberation, her right foot resting on a war god's helmet; she holds the hilt of a broken sword in her right hand, and the broken blade in her left. At the left is inscribed "World" and at the right "War II." Behind the figure are rays of light. On the reverse are inscribed the phrases "Freedom from Fear and Want" and "Freedom of Speech and Religion," separated by a palm branch. Encircling these are the words "United States of America 1941-1945."

The ribbon has a wide center stripe of dark red, edged by two narrow bands of white. At each side is a rainbow pattern—a red center flanked by red-orange, yellow, green, green-blue, and navy blue.

Women's Army Corps Service Medal

Authorized in 1943, this medal was awarded for service in the Women's Army Auxiliary Corps between July 20, 1942, and August 31, 1943, and the Women's Army Corps between September 1, 1943, and September 2, 1945. Since that time, members of the WAC have received the same medals as other members of the Army.

The medal was designed by the Army Heraldic Section. On the obverse is the head of Pallas Athena, goddess of victory and wisdom, in profile, superimposed on a sheathed sword crossed with oak leaves and a palm branch. Above this in a semicircle is inscribed "Women's," with "Army Corps" below. On the reverse, in an arrangement of thirteen stars, a scroll bears the words "For Service in the Women's Auxiliary Corps" in front of the letters "U.S." An eagle perches on the scroll, with wings displayed, and at the bottom is inscribed "1942-1943." (When the WAAC became the WAC it was decided to continue the medal with dates unchanged.)

The ribbon is moss green with gold edges.

OCCUPATION
1945-1955

Army of Occupation Medal

This medal was established in 1946 and the order has been amended several times to cover areas not originally authorized. It is awarded for thirty consecutive days at a normal post of duty on assignment to the armies of occupation.

The medal was designed by the Army Heraldic Section. The obverse shows the Remagen bridge abutments, symbolic of Europe. At the top is the inscription "Army of Occupation" in two lines. The reverse shows Mount Fujiyama, with a cloud near the top, in the background, symbolic of Asia. In front of the mountain are two Japanese junks. Below these is a symbolic wave, and the date "1945" appears at the bottom.

The ribbon is made of equally broad stripes of black (left) and scarlet with narrower white edges. Black and white stand for Germany, and scarlet and white for Japan.

The occupation awards are as follows:

Germany or Austria: For service between May 9, 1945, and May 5, 1955 (exclusive of Berlin). Service with an organization designated by the Department of the Army or individual award of the Berlin Airlift device qualifies the individual for the award.

Austria: For service between May 9, 1945 and July 27, 1955.

Berlin: For service between May 9, 1945, and a terminal date to be announced later.

Italy: For service between May 9, 1945, and September 15, 1947 in the area of Venezia Giulia e Zara or the Province of Udine, or with a designated unit in Italy. Service between May 9 and November 8, 1945 is counted only if the European–African–Middle Eastern Campaign Medal was awarded for service prior to May 9, 1945.

Japan: For service between September 3, 1945, and April 27, 1952. Service between September 3, 1945, and March 2, 1946, is counted only if the Asiatic-Pacific Campaign Medal was awarded for service prior to September 3, 1945. Time is not counted in eligibility if that time meets the requirements of the Korean Service Medal.

Korea: For service between September 3, 1945, and June 29, 1949. Service between September 3, 1945, and March 2, 1946, is counted only if the Asiatic-Pacific Campaign Medal was awarded for service prior to September 3, 1945.

Clasps inscribed "Germany" or "Japan" are issued with the medal to denote occupation duty in those areas. No other clasps are authorized.

The Berlin Airlift device is authorized for ninety consecutive days' service (between June 26, 1948, and September 30, 1949) with an accredited unit. It can also be awarded to an individual by competent field authority. It is a gold-colored metal miniature of a C-54 type aircraft with a ⅜-inch wing span.

Navy Occupation Service Medal

This award was authorized on January 22, 1947, for members of the Navy, Marine Corps, and Coast Guard who participated in the occupation of enemy territories after World War II.

The medal was designed by A. A. Weinman. The obverse shows Neptune riding a mythical animal with a horse's head and a sea serpent's tail. His right hand holds a trident and his left points toward a shore. At the bottom is the inscription "Occupation Service" in two lines. The reverse is the same as that of the Dominican Campaign Medal.

The ribbon is the same as that of the Army of Occupation Medal.

The occupation awards are as follows:

European–African–Middle Eastern Area: For duty from May 8, 1945, on shore in Germany and Austrian territories and from May 8, 1945, to December 15, 1947, in Italian territories. Service in the European–African–Middle Eastern area between May 9 and November 8, 1945, is not credited unless the individual is already eligible for the European–African–Middle Eastern Campaign Medal for service prior to May 8, 1945.

Asiatic-Pacific Area: For duty between September 2, 1945, and April 27, 1952, on shore or on ships in Japanese territories and in parts of Korea and adjacent Korean islands. Service from June 27, 1950, determined to be eligible for the Korean Service Medal is not creditable toward the Navy Occupation Medal. The Navy Occupation Medal is not awarded for any service for which another medal is authorized, except as specified.

Appropriate rectangular clasps, with a rope border, marked "Asia" and "Europe," may be worn on the ribbon.

The Berlin Airlift device is also authorized to be worn on this ribbon by Naval personnel who have served ninety consecutive days or more on duty with an accredited unit.

No one may receive both the Army and Navy medals; persons entitled to both may choose either one.

Medal for Humane Action

This award was authorized on July 20, 1949, for service of at least one hundred and twenty days between June 26, 1948, and September 30, 1949, in the Berlin Airlift or in direct support thereof.

The medal, designed by the Army Heraldic Section, is bronze and measures 1¼ inches in diameter. On the obverse is shown a C-54 airplane. A wreath of wheat at the bottom is centered on the coat of arms of the city of Berlin. The reverse bears an eagle, shield, and arrows from the seal of the Department of Defense. Beneath it are the words "For Humane Action" and above it "To Supply Necessities of Life to the People of Berlin Germany."

The ribbon is light blue with black edges separated from the blue by narrow white stripes. In the center of the blue are narrow stripes of white, red, white.

THE KOREAN WAR
1950-1953

On June 27, 1950, after the North Koreans had unleashed their assault on South Korea across the 38th parallel, the President of the United States announced that American forces were being sent to aid the South Koreans. The Security Council on July 7 adopted a resolution that all UN forces in Korea should act under the UN flag.

By June 25, 1951, the Communists held 2100 square miles less than they had when they started the war. The Korean conflict had reached a stalemate, and had become a war of the trenches, patrols, and hand-to-hand small group battles. For over two years, truce negotiations took place, while the fighting—desperate, bloody, and costly beyond belief—went almost unnoticed. On June 27, 1953, the truce was signed.

The Communists in Korea had had at least 1,500,000 casualties, as well as costly epidemics in their ranks. The UN forces had well over 400,000 men killed, wounded, or missing. Of these, 135,000 were Americans, 260,000 were South Koreans, and 12,000 were from other UN member countries.

Korean Service Medal

This medal was authorized on November 8, 1950, for members of the United States armed forces for service in Korea thirty consecutive or sixty nonconsecutive days between June 27, 1950, and July 27, 1954.

The medal was designed by the Army Heraldic Section. The obverse shows a Korean gateway, encircled by the inscription "Korean Service." On the reverse is a symbol representing the unity of all being, taken from the national flag of Korea. Encircling this is the inscription "United States of America," with a spray of oak at the left joined to a spray of laurel at the right.

The ribbon is light blue with a thin white stripe in the center and narow white edges—the colors of the United Nations.

United Nations Service Medal

This medal was authorized by the United Nations General Assembly on December 12, 1950. The Department of Defense authorized it for the United States Armed Forces on November 27, 1951. It is awarded to officers and enlisted men of the armed forces of the United States who participated in the action in Korea between June 27, 1950, and July 27, 1954. This medal is awarded for any period of time spent in combat.

The medal, in bronze alloy, was designed within the United Nations, along the lines of British medals. The obverse shows the emblem of the United Nations—a polar projection map of the world taken from the North Pole, encircled by olive branches. The reverse of the medal has the inscription "For Service in Defense of the Principles of the Charter of the United Nations" set in five centered lines. The outer edge is a raised rim. A bar which is permanently attached to the medal, and through which the ribbon passes, has the word "Korea" centered thereon.

The ribbon has seventeen equal alternate stripes of pale blue and white with blue at each edge.

National Defense Service Medal

This medal was authorized on April 22, 1953, for officers and enlisted men of the United States armed forces for active-duty service at any time between June 27, 1950, and July 27, 1959.

The medal was designed by the Army Heraldic Section. The obverse shows the American bald eagle, perched on a sword and palm. Above this, in a semicircle, is the inscription "National Defense." The reverse shows a shield, as it appears in the Great Seal of the United States; it is half encircled below with an oak leaf to left and laurel spray to right, knotted in the center.

The ribbon has a wide yellow stripe in the center, flanked by narrow stripes of red, white, blue, white, wide red stripes.

If a member of the service has previously been awarded this medal, and remained in service after July 1960, a bronze star (Navy) or a bronze oak leaf (Army and Air Force), worn centered upon the ribbon, signifies service during the Vietnam conflict.

EXPEDITIONARY MEDALS

Marine Corps Expeditionary Ribbon

Authorized in 1919, this ribbon was the forerunner of the Marine Corp Expeditionary Medal.

It has a scarlet center flanked by stripes of gold, with narrow scarlet edges. These are the colors of the Marine Corps, though the gold is often mistaken for khaki.

On March 1, 1920, bronze numerals were authorized to be worn in the center of the ribbon to denote the number of expeditions in which the wearer had participated. This was a unique feature in decorations.

Marine Corps Expeditionary Medal

This medal was authorized on March 1, 1929, for members of the Marine Corps who have engaged in operations against armed opposition on foreign territory, or have served in circumstances which merit special recognition but for which no campaign medal is awarded.

The obverse, designed by Walker Hancock, shows a Marine in the uniform of the 1920s under full pack, charging with fixed bayonet. Above, in a semicircle, is the inscription "Expeditions," and at the base are wave scrolls. The reverse is the same as that of the Marine Corps Dominican Campaign Medal.

The ribbon is the same as the Expeditionary Ribbon.

The places and dates of expeditions for which this medal is awarded to the Marine Corps and to the Navy are: Abyssinia, 1903; Argentina, 1890; Chile, 1891; China, 1894–1895, 1898, 1911, 1924–1929, 1937; Colombia, 1885, 1895, 1901–1904; Cuba, 1912; Dominican Republic, 1903–1904, 1914, 1916, 1918; Egypt, 1882; Haiti, 1891, 1914–1915, 1918, 1920, 1929; Hawaiian Islands, 1874, 1889, 1893; Honduras, 1903, 1907, 1924; Korea, 1888, 1894–1895, 1904; Nicaragua, 1894, 1896, 1898–1899, 1909–1910, 1912, 1918, 1926; Panama, 1873, 1885, 1895,

1901–1904; Philippine Islands, 1911; Russia, 1905; Samoa, 1888, 1899; Siberia, 1920; Syria, 1903; Turkey, 1921–1922; Wake Island, 1941.

Originally, numerals were worn upon the ribbon to indicate the number of expeditions in which the wearer took part. Later a bronze star was authorized for each expedition. The only exception to this was a small $\frac{3}{16}$-inch silver "W" to be worn on the service ribbon by men who served in the defense of Wake Island, December 7 to 22, 1941. On the ribbon of the medal this is replaced by a bar inscribed "Wake Island." This medal has also been awarded to Marine personnel for service in Cuba, Lebanon, and the Congo during the Cold War period, 1954-1965.

When the present supply of Marine Corps Expeditionary Medals is exhausted, the Navy Expeditionary Medal will be the only one awarded to either Navy or Marine Corps personnel for participation in expeditions.

Navy Expeditionary Medal

This medal was authorized on August 15, 1936, for officers and enlisted men of the Navy who have engaged in operations against an armed enemy on foreign territory or for those who have served in circumstances which merit special recognition but for which no campaign medal is awarded.

The medal was designed by A. A. Weinman. The obverse shows an armed sailor, in water to his knees, beaching a boat containing an officer and Marines with weapons, and an American flag. Above this scene, in a semicircle, is the word "Expeditions." The reverse is the same as that of the Navy Dominican Campaign Medal.

The ribbon has a broad blue center stripe, flanked by equal yellow stripes, with narrow blue stripes at the edges.

For personnel taking part in additional expeditions, a ¼-inch bronze star is added to the suspension ribbon and service ribbon bar. The only exception is the silver "W" and medal clasp authorized to defenders of Wake Island. This medal has also been awarded to Navy personnel for service in Cuba, Lebanon, and the Congo during the Cold War period, 1954-1965.

This medal may become obsolete with the issue of the Armed Forces Expeditionary Medal.

Armed Forces Expeditionary Medal

This is the newest service medal; it was established on December 4, 1961, for award to members of the United States armed forces who, after July 1, 1958, have participated in a United States military operation and encountered foreign armed opposition, or were in danger of hostile action by foreign armed forces.

The obverse has an eagle with wings raised, perched on a sword. In back of this is a compass rose, with rays coming from the angles of the compass points. This design is encircled by the inscription "Armed Forces" at the top and "Expeditionary Service" below. Between these words, completing the circle, is a sprig of laurel on each side.

The reverse has the shield as it appears in the President's seal. Below this are branches of laurel to right and left, joined in the center by a knot. At the top, in a semicircle, is the inscription "United States of America."

It is believed that this medal will recognize service in such places as South Vietnam, Laos, Lebanon, the Congo, and Quemoy, Matsu, and the Formosa Straits.

PART THREE
AWARDS TO CIVILIANS

AIRMEN AND EXPLORERS

NC-4 Medal

This award was authorized as a large gold medal on February 9, 1929, and as a bronze "miniature" (actually the usual medal size) on April 25, 1935, for the men of the NC-4 flying boat which made the first transatlantic flight in 1919.

The NC-4 was one of three flying boats which started out from Newfoundland on May 16, 1919. (The NC-2 had been damaged by fire and removed from the squadron.) The NC-1 and NC-3 were forced down on the ocean by heavy fog; the NC-1 broke apart in the huge waves after her crew was rescued, and the NC-3 sailed 205 miles to the Azores. The NC-4, after stops in the Azores and Ponta Delgado, landed in Lisbon on May 27.

The medal was designed by Catherine G. Barton. The original, in gold, was not designed for wear. The obverse shows a gull flying over waves, with the inscription "First Transatlantic Flight United States Navy May 1919" in a semicircle above. The reverse has a circular inscription. The upper half reads, "J. H. Towers, A. C. Read, E. F. Stone, H. C. Rodd, J. J. Breese, F. Rhodes." Commander J. H. Towers was the squadron chief; the other names are those of men who belonged to the crew of the NC-4. The lower half reads, "Presented by the President of the United States in the Name of Congress." Within this is a circular plaque inscribed "NC-4," with "Newfoundland" above and "Portugal" below.

The miniature, an exact copy of the large gold medal, was later authorized for wear. The ribbon for this has equal stripes—red, white, blue, green, red. Red, white, and blue symbolize the United States, and green and red are the national colors of Portugal.

Peary Polar Expedition Medal, 1908-1909

On January 28, 1944, Congress authorized a medal for members of Admiral Robert E. Peary's polar expedition of 1908-1909. Peary had made two attempts to reach the North Pole (in 1902 and 1905-1906) before his successful journey in 1909. He reached the Pole on April 6 of that year with a Negro named Matthew Henson and four Eskimos named Coqueeh, Ootah, Eginwah, and Seeglo. The last two survivors of that trip, Matthew Henson and Ootah, died in 1945.

The medal, designed by John R. Sinnock, has on the obverse a bust of Admiral Peary in hooded parka, over the inscription "Peary Polar Expedition 1908-09." This design is within a circular plaque set upon a compass rose of sixteen points, the top (north) one a fleur-de-lis. The reverse is divided into three equal horizontal sections. The top section has a flowing American flag between two sled dogs. The center part has the inscription "Presented in the name of Congress in Recognition of the Efforts and Services of the Peary Polar Expedition of 1908-09 in the Field of Science and for the Cause of Polar Exploration by Aiding the Discovery of the North Pole by Admiral Peary." The bottom section has a space appropriate for the inscription of the recipient's name, with a pair of snow shoes below.

The ribbon is ivory, with ¼-inch stripes of turquoise near each edge.

Byrd Arctic Expedition Medal, 1926

A bill was passed by the House of Representatives on August 6, 1962, and is now being considered by the Senate, to award a medal to the members of Richard E. Byrd's Arctic Expedition of 1926. During that expedition Commander Byrd and Floyd Bennett made the first flight over the North Pole (for which they were both awarded the Medal of Honor by special legislation).

Byrd Antarctic Expedition Medal, 1928-1930

This medal was authorized on May 23, 1930, for members of the Byrd Antarctic Expedition which left the United States in September 1928 and reached Antarctica in December. There Byrd established a base of operations which he called Little America. On November 29 he made the first flight over the South Pole.

The medal, designed by Francis H. Packer, was cast in gold for Admiral Byrd, in silver for his officers, and in bronze for other personnel. The obverse shows Admiral Byrd, in parka and flying helmet, holding a ski pole. There is an ice formation in the right background. Around the edge of the medal is the inscription "Byrd Antarctic Expedition 1928 1930." The reverse shows a ship under full sail above a panel which is inscribed "Presented to the Officers and Men of the Byrd Expedition to Express the High Admiration in Which the Congress and the American People Hold Their Heroic and Undaunted Services in Connection with the Scientific Investigations and Extraordinary Aerial Exploration on the Antarctic Continent." Below this is a trimotored airplane in front view, of the type that Byrd used to circle the South Pole.

The ribbon has an ice-blue center stripe, flanked by narrower silver-white stripes.

Second Byrd Antarctic Expedition Medal, 1933-1935

This medal was authorized on June 2, 1936, for all personnel of the Second Byrd Expedition who spent the winter night (six months) at Little America or who commanded either of the expedition ships.

The medal, designed by Heinz Warnicke, is of silver. Its obverse shows Admiral Byrd, in parka and snow boots, petting an Eskimo dog at his right and holding a ski pole in his left hand. In the background are ice formations. At the right are the dates "1933 1935," and encircling the scene are the words "Byrd Antarctic Expedition." The reverse has a panel in the center with the inscription "Presented to the Officers and Men of the Second Byrd Antarctic Expedition, to Express the Very High Admiration in Which the

113 ⬧

Congress and the American People Hold Their Heroic and Undaunted Accomplishments for Science Unequaled in the History
of Polar Exploration." At the left is a view of the Little America
radio towers, and at the right is a sailing ship. Above the panel
is a trimotored airplane, and below are a dog sled and team.

The ribbon is plain white grosgrain.

United States Antarctic Expedition Medal, 1939-1941

This medal was authorized on September 24, 1945, for members
of the First United States Antarctic Expedition of 1939-1941,
commanded by Admiral Byrd. The expedition was not named
after Byrd because it was an official government operation. Byrd's
previous explorations had been privately financed.

The medal was designed by John R. Sinnock. The lower half
of the obverse shows a partial map with the names "South Pacific
Ocean, Little America, South Pole, Antarctica, and Palmerland."
Above this is a three-part scroll inscribed, "Science, Pioneering,
Exploration." Around the edge is the inscription "The United
States Antarctic Expedition 1939 1941." On the reverse, "By Act
of Congress of the United States of America to" is set in four lines,
over a blank space for the recipient's name. Below is the inscrip-
tion "In Recognition of Invaluable Service to This Nation by
Courageous Pioneering in Polar Exploration Which Resulted in
Important Geographical and Scientific Discoveries," in seven lines.

The ribbon has three equal stripes—ice blue, white, ice blue—
and the white center stripe has two narrow stripes near each
edge.

Antarctica Service Medal

This medal was authorized in July 1961 and the design received
final approval in 1963. It is awarded to members of Antarctic expeditions and personnel of the permanent Antarctica stations,

starting with the United States Navy operation "Highjump" under the late Rear Admiral Byrd in 1946 and 1947. It is awarded to officers and enlisted men of the armed forces and to deserving civilians, such as scientists and polar experts.

The medal, designed by the United States Mint, is a green-gold disc. On the obverse is a heroic figure of a man in Antarctic clothing, with hood thrown back, arms extended, hands closed, and legs spread, to symbolize stability, determination, courage, and devotion. The figure stands on broken ground, with clouds in the background and mountains in the far distance. The reverse shows a polar projection map of the Antarctic Continent, across which are the words "Courage Sacrifice Devotion" set in three centered lines, all within a symbolic circular border of penguins and marine life.

The proposed ribbon has a white center stripe flanked by progressively darker shades of blue, with black at the edges.

THE MERCHANT MARINE

Men and ships of the United States Merchant Marine participated in every invasion and landing operation of World War II and the Korean conflict. Even before Pearl Harbor they were being bombed and torpedoed as they moved supplies to our allies. Since most ships early in the war had no defense against submarines, they traveled in convoys of some fifty each, protected by destroyers and other escorts. Convoy duty was boring at best, and was often extremely dangerous, especially on the Atlantic and on the "Murmansk Run" past the Scandinavian peninsula. The Maritime Commission created its own awards for its courageous men.

Members of the Merchant Marine were entitled to the awards of the Philippine government—the Philippine Liberation Medal and the Philippine Defense Bar.

Merchant Marine Distinguished Service Medal

This medal is the Merchant Services' highest award for heroism. Congress, on April 11, 1943, authorized the Maritime Commission to award it to any person in the American Merchant Marine who, on or after September 3, 1939, has distinguished himself by outstanding service in the line of duty. For World War II, 145 of these medals were awarded, 30 posthumously.

The striking design, by Paul Manship, was approved by the Fine Arts Commission on July 31, 1945. The obverse is a silver compass rose of eight points, each tipped with a ball, imposed upon a bronze compass card. The reverse has a disk within the compass rose, charged with a shield of the United States Coat of Arms, with the words "Distinguished Service" above the shield and "United States Merchant Marine" encircling the whole. The medal is suspended from a swivel in the form of an eagle in front of crossed anchors under an arch of leaves.

The ribbon has a broad red center stripe, flanked by narrower stripes of white, with broad edges of dark blue.

A bronze lapel device is also awarded for civilian wear. It is a ¼-inch compass rose, with eight points, upon a compass card.

Meritorious Service Medal

This medal was authorized on August 29, 1944, for any member, officer, or master of an American ship or any foreign ship operated for the United States Maritime Commission or the War Shipping Administration, who is commended by the administrator for meritorious conduct not of such a nature as to warrant the Distinguished Service Medal. There were 424 of these medals awarded for action during World War II, 16 posthumously.

This beautiful bronze medal, designed by Paul Manship, shows, on the obverse, an eagle perched on the flukes of an anchor, with a laurel branch in its claws. Encircling this are the words "For Meritorious Service in the United States Merchant Marine." The center area is blank, suitable for engraving.

The ribbon is blue with a center stripe of darker blue, flanked by narrow stripes of white, red, and yellow.

The Mariner's Medal

This award was established on May 10, 1943, for any seaman who, while serving on a ship of the Merchant Service, is wounded, undergoes physical injury, or suffers through dangerous exposure as a result of an act of the enemy of the United States.

Designed by Paul Manship, it is a wide eight-pointed gilt cross with a large silver medallion in the center of the obverse, on which is an eagle standing on an anchor. The reverse has the inscription "United States" above and "Merchant Marine" below, forming a circle. In the center are a wreath and a hand carrying a blazing torch above waves.

The ribbon has a narrow white center stripe, flanked by red on the left and blue on the right.

Gallant Ship Medallion and Citation Plaque

An Executive Order of August 29, 1944, authorized the administrator of the War Shipping Administration to award a plaque to any United States or foreign ship operated by or for the United States Maritime Commission of the War Shipping Administration which, after September 8, 1939, has served "in outstanding action against attack from the enemy or in gallant action in marine disasters or other emergencies at sea." Nine of these awards were given for action during World War II, and one for the Korean war. There have been four postwar awards.

Gallant Ship Citation Bar

Officers and seamen who have served on such a ship are awarded this bar. It is a service ribbon of the usual size—1⅜ inches by ⅜ inches, colored dark sea green with narrow white edges. In the center is a small silver seahorse. (Color plate III, no. 39.)

The Combat Bar

This award was authorized on May 10, 1943, for members of the Merchant Marine who served on a ship when it was attacked or damaged by the enemy or an instrumentality of war, such as mines. The bar has three horizontal stripes of (from top to bottom) purple, red, and blue, separated by two white stripes. A silver star is worn upon the ribbon for each time the wearer has been forced to abandon ship. (Color plate II, no. 41.)

The following awards are all ribbons; they were presented to officers and seamen for service in various theatres of war.

Merchant Marine Defense Bar

This award was created on August 24, 1944, for members of the crews of United States merchant ships between September 8, 1939, and December 7, 1941.

It is a service ribbon of the usual size, with a black center which gradually blends into bright magenta and then to white, with a dark green stripe at each edge. (Color plate II, no. 42.)

Atlantic War Zone Bar
This was authorized on May 10, 1943, for officers and seamen of ships operated by or for the War Shipping Administration for service in the Atlantic War Zone, including the North Atlantic, South Atlantic, Gulf of Mexico, Caribbean Sea, Barents Sea, and Greenland Sea.

It has a center stripe of flame red, edged with white which gradually blends into light red edges. (Color plate II, no. 43.)

Mediterranean–Middle East War Zone Bar
Created on May 10, 1943, this ribbon is awarded for service in the war zone which included the Mediterranean Sea, the Red Sea, the Arabian Sea, and the Indian Ocean west of 80 degrees east longitude.

It has narrow stripes of green, white, and green in the center, flanked by two wider yellow bands, and stripes of red, white, and blue at each edge. (Color plate II, no. 44.)

Pacific War Zone Bar
Created on May 10, 1943, for service in the war zone that included the North Pacific, South Pacific, and the Indian Ocean east of 80 degrees east longitude.

It has a center stripe of red flanked by stripes of white and blue; at the outer edges are wide bands of red blending into yellow-orange. (Color plate II, no. 45.)

Merchant Marine Victory Medal

This award was created on August 8, 1946, for service on any vessel operated by or for the Maritime Commission or the War Shipping Administration for thirty days between December 7, 1941, and September 3, 1945.

Designed by Paul Manship, it is a round bronze medal. The obverse shows a female figure holding a trident in her right hand and an olive branch in her left. At the left is the word "World" and at the right "War II." At the bottom, in the background, is the conning tower of an enemy submarine. The reverse shows a fouled anchor with a scroll on it inscribed *"Firmitas Adversaria Superat."* Surrounding this is a border inscribed, in large letters, "United States Merchant Marine 1941-1945."

The ribbon has wide red edges, and a red center flanked by narrow stripes of white, then blue, green, and yellow.

Korean War Service-Bar

Created on July 24, 1956, this bar is awarded to officers and seamen who served aboard merchant vessels flying the American flag in waters adjacent to Korea between June 30, 1950, and September 30, 1953.

It is a service ribbon of the usual size, with a center stripe of blue blending into white, then into a watered stripe of red, and again into white at the edges. (Color plate III, no. 42.)

OTHER CIVILIAN AWARDS

Many people not in uniform served the United States gallantly and courageously in World War II. The home and defense fronts were as important to the prosecution of the war as the men who maneuvered and fought the battles. In recognition of this, a series of awards was created expressly for civilians.

Medal for Merit

This medal was authorized on July 20, 1942, by the President of the United States for civilians of nations waging war under a joint declaration with the United States, and to civilians of other friendly foreign nations who distinguish themselves by the performance of outstanding services. This medal is not being awarded at the present time, and will not be awarded until the President so directs. It is comparable to the Distinguished Service Medal.

It was designed by Colonel Townsend Heard, and the sculptor was Katharine W. Lane. The obverse shows an American eagle facing left, with outspread wings, standing on a sheaf of arrows with points down. In front of this is the motto *"Novus Ordo Seclorum,"* taken from the reverse of the Great Seal. This design, in gold-colored metal, rests on an open circle of blue enamel with thirteen stars in white. The eagle's wings spread beyond the circle, and the sheaf of arrows extends below it. The reverse has the inscription "United States of America" around the top, and at the bottom "For Merit," with sprays of laurel at each side. The back of the eagle is fully molded. The medal is suspended from the ribbon by a green enamel laurel wreath.

The magenta silk ribbon has two narrow white stripes near the center.

Medal of Freedom

This medal, authorized on July 6, 1945, and amended on April 3, 1953, is awarded to any person who, on or after December 7, 1941, has aided the United States in war against an enemy, or has furthered the interest of United States security or that of an ally during a national emergency. It is not awarded for service performed within the United States or to a member of the armed forces of the United States.

The obverse has the head, shoulders, and headdress of Freedom derived from the statue on the United States Capitol dome in Washington. This faces to the left. In the lower portion is the word "Freedom." The reverse has the "Liberty Bell," centered, encircled by the inscription "United States of America." The designer is not known.

The ribbon is bright claret (as for the Legion of Merit), with four narrow white stripes near the center. These colors are the same as that of the Medal for Merit, and this award is considered a junior grade of that medal.

This medal is awarded to citizens and members of the Armed Forces of foreign nations in four degrees, corresponding to certain American military decorations. Three are in the form of palms to be worn on the suspension ribbon. They are: Gold Palm (equivalent to the Legion of Merit, Chief Commander); Silver Palm (Legion of Merit, Commander); Bronze Palm (Legion of Merit, Officer and Legionnaire); and without palm (Bronze Star Medal). Citizens of the United States are awarded it only without palm.

The National Security Medal

This award was authorized on January 19, 1953, for any person regardless of nationality, who, on or after July 26, 1947, has contributed to the national intelligence effort of the United States. This medal has been awarded very rarely. One of the recipients, the late William J. Donovan (winner of the Medal of Honor in World War I) received it in April 1957 for work at director of the Office of Strategic Service (OSS).

The medal was designed by the United States Mint. The obverse has a blue enameled compass rose of sixteen points surrounded by a red enameled oval in which the words "United States of America" appear across the top and "National Security" at the bottom, in gold. The whole is enclosed within a laurel wreath of gold-finished bronze and is surmounted by an American bald eagle standing with wings raised, facing left. The reverse has the words "Presented to" on the compass rose above a blank area suitable for engraving. The laurel wreath is raised, as on the obverse.

The ribbon is dark blue with a gold diagonal ladder pattern in the center.

President's Award for Distinguished
Federal Civilian Service

This award, created on June 27, 1957, is the highest recognition for civilian career officers and federal government employees. It may be awarded for long and distinguished career service, but generally five awards are made each year for the best achievements in improving government service or serving the public interest.

The medal, designed by the United States Mint, is a gold ellipse. On the obverse is an American eagle with wings displayed and inverted, surrounded by a laurel wreath which forms the outer edge of the medal. The reverse is inscribed "Award of the President of the United States to" set in four lines, with a space for the recipient's name, followed by "For Distinguished Federal Civilian Service" set in three lines.

The decoration is worn on a neck ribbon which has a wide center stripe of dark blue, with thin stripes of white and light blue at either edge.

Navy Distinguished Public Service Award

Originally a certificate and lapel button, this medal was not presented until July 1951. It is the highest recognition that the Secretary of the Navy may pay to a civilian. It is given to citizens of the United States not employed by the Department of the Navy

for the period for which the award was recommended, who make special contributions "bearing directly on the accomplishment of the Navy's mission."

The medal, designed by the United States Mint, is solid gold. The obverse has the seal of the Navy Department, encircled by the inscription "Navy Department" above and "United States of America" below. The reverse has the words "Awarded to," above a blank tablet, suitable for inscription of the recipient's name, resting on a spray of laurel. Arched at the top of the medal is the word "Distinguished"; set horizontally below the tablet is the word "Public," and arched along the bottom edge is the word "Service."

The ribbon is half blue (on the left) and half golden-yellow, the colors of the United States Navy.

The circular lapel button has a fouled anchor with the letters "U.S.N.," all encircled by the inscription "Distinguished Public Service."

Distinguished Civilian Service Medal

This medal was authorized on September 17, 1956, to provide distinctive recognition of valuable public service in the national interest. It is awarded to civilians not employed by the government who have rendered meritorious service to the Department of Defense, the Secretary of Defense, or one of the military departments since July 26, 1947.

The medal is a gold-colored disk. Centered on it is a triangle with one point up, behind an American eagle with outspread wings and a shield on its breast. The lower edge of the medal is lined with a laurel wreath. The reverse has the inscription "To" over a blank space suitable for the recipient's name, and "For Distinguished Public Service to the Department of Defense" below.

The ribbon is white, with separated stripes of blue, red, blue near each edge.

Outstanding Civilian Service Medal

This award is a junior grade of the Distinguished Civilian Service Medal.

The medal, of bronze, was designed by the United States Mint. The obverse has a triangle with one point up; upon this is an eagle, with wings outspread and a shield on its breast. A laurel wreath encircles the lower outer edge of the medal.

The reverse has the inscription "To" on a blank space, suitable for engraving recipient's name, and "For Outstanding Public Service to the Department of Defense" below.

The ribbon has thirteen alternating stripes of white and red, with white ones at either edge. The white stripes have pin stripes of blue centered within them.

Exceptional Civilian Service Award

This decoration is awarded to any United States civilian not em-ployed by the government, who has rendered exceptional services to the Department of the Army. It may also be awarded to any civilian, United States or foreign, not employed by the government, for an act of heroism involving voluntary risk of life.

This gold-colored medal was designed by the United States Mint. Its outer edge is encircled by a laurel wreath. Centered in the obverse is the American eagle as it appears on the Great Seal, with wings outspread and a shield on its breast. In its left claw is a group of arrows, and in its right a laurel branch. Above is a display of thirteen stars in a circle of clouds.

The reverse is engraved with the recipient's name.

The ribbon is cornflower blue with three dotted white lines in the center.

Air Force Exceptional Service Award

This decoration, authorized on August 30, 1948, is awarded to United States civilians, not employed by the government, who distinguish themselves by exceptional services rendered to the Department of the Air Force. It may also be awarded to any

civilian, United States or foreign, not employed by the government, for an act of heroism involving voluntary risk of life.

The award, designed by the United States Mint, is a circular gold-colored medal bearing the Air Force coat of arms on the obverse. It has a shield with eagle-claw baton, centered upon four crossed lightning bolts, and wings. Above this is an American eagle, wings outspread, perched on a baton. Behind the eagle is a symbolic cloud design. A laurel wreath encircles the outer edge of the medal.

The reverse is engraved with the recipient's name.

The ribbon is dark blue with three dotted golden-orange lines in the center.

Meritorious Civilian Service Award

This decoration is a junior award of the Exceptional Civilian Service Award and is given for service that does not warrant the higher decoration.

It is of the same design and size as the senior award, but is in bronze.

The ribbon is cornflower blue, with three white pin stripes in the center.

Distinguished Service Medal of the National Aeronautics and Space Administration

This medal was originated on July 29, 1959, by the NASA Civilian Space Agency to reward achievements by employees of the NASA as well as by those attached temporarily to its projects. It is awarded for personal heroism or endurance, scientific achievement, high levels of leadership, and administrative accomplishments. The first recipient was John W. Crowley, to whom it was given on June 30, 1959, "for outstanding leadership in aeronautics." Perhaps the most widely known recipients have been the astronauts who pioneered in space travel.

The medal, in gold, was designed by the United States Mint. The obverse shows the official seal of the NASA—a planet with

a natural satellite, and another planet in the distance. In the fore-front from lower left to upper right is a wing-type satellite, and in the background are numerous stars. All this is within a circle bearing the inscription "National Aeronautics and Space Administration U.S.A." These words and the two edges of the circle are raised and highly polished, and the depressed portions are frosted in contrast. The reverse has a wreath at the edges formed of two branches of oak leaves, joined at the bottom by two acorns. Slightly above the center, within the wreath, is the inscription "Distinguished Service." There is a blank area for the recipient's name.

The ribbon has a thin white center stripe, flanked by equally wide stripes of light blue, medium blue, dark blue, and navy blue.

Other medals of the National Aeronautics and Space Administration are to be designed by the Army Heraldic Section, subject to approval by NASA and the commission of Fine Arts. These are:

The NASA Medal for Outstanding Leadership: For leadership which has had a pronounced effect upon the aerospace technological or administrative programs of NASA.

The NASA Medal for Exceptional Scientific Achievement: For unusually significant scientific or engineering accomplishments which contribute to the programs of the NASA, the Department of Defense, or other government agencies.

The NASA Medal for Exceptional Bravery: For courageous handling of an emergency in NASA activities by an individual who has acted to safeguard the loss of human life or government property, or who has performed, irrespective of personal danger, an official task of great importance to the mission of NASA.

Selective Service Medal

This award was authorized on July 2, 1945, for uncompensated personnel of the Selective Service System for two or more years of

service in the states and territories of the United States, and to such other personnel as may be selected by the Director of Selective Service.

The medal, designed by the United States Mint, bears on the obverse the seal of the Selective Service System. An eagle, as on the Great Seal of the United States, has a shield on its breast bearing the letters "SSS" and holds arrows in its left claw and a branch of laurel in its right. Above the eagle are thirteen stars. The design is encircled by the inscription "Selective Service System World War II." The reverse is plain, except for the inscription "Awarded in the Name of the Congress of the United States for Faithful and Loyal Service."

The ribbon has a wide navy-blue center stripe, on either side of which are broad stripes of orange-yellow, each divided by a narrow stripe of navy blue.

American Typhus Commission Medal

This award was authorized on December 24, 1942, for meritorious service in connection with the work of the Typhus Control Commission.

The medal was designed by Edmond R. Amateis. The obverse shows the profiles of Charles J. H. Nicolle (1866-1936), and Howard Taylor Ricketts (1871-1910), who contributed to knowledge of the cause and transmission of typhus fever. Completely encircling these profiles is the inscription "Charles Nicolle Howard Taylor Ricketts." The reverse has the staff of Aesculapius on the right, and behind it the inscription "United States of America Typhus Commission for Meritorious Service." There is a small area between the words "for" and "Meritorious Service," suitable for engraving.

The ribbon has three equal stripes—golden yellow in the center and purple-red at each side.

Presidential Medal of Freedom

This new medal, the highest honor the President of the United States can confer on civilians in peacetime, was established by executive order in 1957 and amended in 1963. It is to be awarded annually to Americans who make exceptional contributions toward national security, the national interest, world peace, culture, or "other significant public and private endeavors." On July 4, 1963, in the first annual Independence Day honors list, President Kennedy named thirty-one persons—among them the first Negroes and the first women to be so honored—to receive the award. The decorations were not actually presented to the recipients until after the President's death in November 1963.

The medal was designed by the Army Institute of Heraldry under the direction of President Kennedy, who added his own touches to the final specifications. It consists of a large white enameled star, in the center of which is a circular blue field with thirteen silver stars. The white star is mounted on a red shield, visible between the arms, with a gold eagle, wings spread, in each of the interstices. The medal is suspended by a loop of gold braid from a blue silk ribbon bordered in white. It is worn as either a neck or a breast decoration.

The medal was awarded to President Kennedy posthumously.

Supplement, 1970

INTRODUCTORY NOTE

American War Medals and Decorations first appeared in 1964, and since that time it has become the standard reference work in its field. Since the first appearance of this book, a number of new decorations and medals have been created—new decorations for the Air Force and Coast Guard, three new campaign medals for the Vietnam conflict, and a whole new series of NASA awards reflecting the growth of this agency and advances in the aerospace field. The first edition of this book has gone through four printings since 1964. Meanwhile, the number of decorations and medals to be included in any such up-to-date work has been increased by more than twenty.

Clearly, to maintain the standard of this book as a reference tool and to do full homage to these awards, revisions and additions must be made. The author and the publishers have decided that recent changes and additions should be incorporated as a supplement to *American War Medals and Decorations*. It is our hope that this supplement will do full justice to the men so recently honored by their country, and will further acquaint the reader with the newest American decorations and medals.

MEDAL OF HONOR
Air Force

This was established by Congress on July 6, 1960, as the highest of several awards created specifically for the Air Force. It is given in the name of Congress to officers and enlisted men who distinguished themselves by gallantry and intrepidity at the risk of their lives, above and beyond the call of duty, in action involving actual combat with an armed enemy of the United States.

The medal is a gold-finished star, its five points tipped with trefoils. In each point of the star are two stylized gold wings, with enameled green background. The head of the Statue of Liberty in the center is surrounded by thirty-four gold stars. The star is surrounded by a laurel wreath, enameled green and edged in gold. The medal is suspended from a gold design, taken from the Air Force coat of arms, which shows a center baton with eagle claw ends resting on a pair of aviator's wings emitting thunderbolts from the center. This in turn is attached to a horizontal bar bearing the word "Valor." Through the bar is the neck of the ribbon, which at the center has an octagonal pad of the traditional light blue moiré with thirteen white stars. Behind this passes the neck ribbon of light blue. The reverse is blank and suitable for engraving name, rank, and date of action for which the award is given.

The first presentation of this Medal of Honor was made at the White House in Washington on January 19, 1967, when the President placed it around the neck of Major Bernard F. Fisher, United States Air Force. According to the citation, Major Fisher "distinguished himself by conspicuous gallantry and intrepidity at the risk of his life above and beyond the call of duty as an A-1E pilot near A Shau, Republic of Vietnam, on 10 March 1966. . . . Hostile troops had surrounded the Special Forces camp and were continuously raking it with automatic weapons fire from the surrounding hills. . . . During the battle, Major Fisher observed a fellow airman crash-land on the battle-torn airstrip . . . Directing his own air cover, he landed his aircraft and taxied almost the full length of the runway, which was littered with the debris and parts of an exploded aircraft. While effecting a successful rescue of the downed pilot, heavy ground fire was observed, with nineteen bullets striking his aircraft. In the face of the withering ground fire, he applied power and gained enough speed to lift-off at the over-run of the airstrip."

Major Fisher has also earned the Distinguished Flying Cross, Air Medal (with eight oak leaf clusters), Combat Readiness Medal, AF Commendation Medal, American Campaign Medal, National Defense Service Medal, Armed Forces Expeditionary Medal, Vietnam Service Medal, Air Force Longevity Service Award Ribbon, and the Small Arms Expert Marksmanship Ribbon.

DISTINGUISHED SERVICE MEDAL
Air Force

This decoration, established by Congress on July 6, 1960, is awarded to members of the United States Air Force who distinguish themselves by exceptionally meritorious service to the government in a duty of great responsibility, in combat or otherwise.

The sunburst design is one of the most striking examples of the medalist's art. A semiprecious blue stone is the center of thirteen pointed gold rays separated by thirteen five-pointed stars enameled white and edged in gold. The reverse is plain, suitable for engraving the recipient's name, rank, and date of action. The medal is suspended from the ribbon by a wide slotted bar, the center of which incorporates a wing design. The ribbon has a wide center stripe of white, flanked by narrow gold stripes, wide blue stripes, and narrow gold stripes at the edge.

This decoration was designed by the Institute of Heraldry. The center stone represents the vault of the heavens; the thirteen stars represent the original colonies and man's chain of achievements. The sunburst represents the glory that accompanies great achievements, and the rays depict man's quest for light and knowledge.

JOINT SERVICE COMMENDATION MEDAL
Department of Defense

This decoration, established by the Department of Defense on June 25, 1963, is awarded by the office of the Secretary of Defense, the Joint Chiefs of Staff, and other Department of Defense agencies or joint activities reporting through the Joint Chiefs of Staff. Any member of the Armed Forces who distinguishes himself by meritorious achievement or service while serving in any specified activity after January 1, 1965, is eligible for this award. However, it will not be awarded for any period of service for which any of the Commendation Medals of the branches of the Armed Forces are given.

The medal consists of four conjoined hexagons of green enamel. Centered on this is an eagle in gold with outspread wings, grasping three arrows in its talons (as depicted on the seal of the Department of Defense). Above the eagle are thirteen gold stars, and at the base is a gold stylized heraldic delineation representing land, sea, and air. This design is enclosed by a circular wreath of laurel bound with bands, also in gold. The reverse has a tablet in the center, suitable for engraving, and the words "FOR MILITARY MERIT." At the bottom is a sprig of laurel.

The ribbon has a center stripe of laurel green, on either side of which are stripes of white, green, and white, and, at the edges, wide stripes of light blue.

NAVY ACHIEVEMENT MEDAL

This award, authorized by the Secretary of the Navy on January 24, 1962, ranks just below the Navy Commendation Medal and is awarded to junior officers or enlisted personnel serving in any capacity with the Navy or Marine Corps (except foreign personnel) who distinguish themselves by outstanding professional achievement or leadership. It is interesting to note that it is given for leadership only to enlisted men. The decoration is for noncombat service only.

The medal, designed by the Institute of Heraldry, consists of an octagonal tablet with raised surface. At each corner of the inner rectangle appears a five-pointed star. In the center of the tablet is an old-style fouled naval anchor. The reverse of the medal is blank and suitable for engraving.

The ribbon for the medal, almost identical to that of the Navy Commendation Medal, is laurel green with two wide stripes of orange near each side.

NAVY MERITORIOUS UNIT COMMENDATION RIBBON

This award, established by the Secretary of the Navy on April 15, 1968, with the approval of the President, is conferred on any ship, aircraft, detachment, or other unit in the Naval Service of the United States to recognize valor and meritorious performance by a unit under either combat or non-combat conditions, but not of a degree sufficient to justify the awarding of the Navy Unit Commendation Ribbon, which it ranks immediately behind. The service rendered must be comparable to that which would merit the awarding of a Bronze Star medal. It is awarded in the name of the Secretary of the Navy.

The ribbon has a broad stripe of hunter green at either side, and in the center equal stripes of yellow, red, yellow, blue, and yellow. All personnel attached to a unit and actually present and serving during the time the unit is commended are authorized to wear the ribbon permanently.

AIR FORCE COMBAT READINESS MEDAL

This medal was originally created as a personal decoration, but its status has since been changed to that of a service award. It now takes precedence over the Air Force Good Conduct Medal. Established by the Secretary of the Air Force in 1965, it is awarded to members of the Air Force manning weapons systems whose primary wartime mission required delivery of weapons against hostile targets. Service in this combat-ready status must have been for at least 120 consecutive days, unless a break in the continuous service was not due to any instance of nonprofessionalism. Special duty with other United States military service can be creditable, provided the man is in a combat-ready status with that service.

This striking medal shows an inverted triangle on top of a delta-swept winglike object, both representing supersonic fighters. The whole is enclosed by a stylized compass rose with triangles at the points, indicating the world-wide nature of the mission. The reverse has a blank area in the center, with the inscription, "For combat readiness Air Force" in a circle near the edge.

The ribbon has a wide center stripe of red, flanked by narrow bands of light blue, dark blue, and light blue again, and narrow red stripes at the edges.

NAVAL RESERVE MERITORIOUS SERVICE MEDAL

Originally authorized by the Secretary of the Navy in a 1960 report, this consisted of only a ribbon. A Navy notice on June 25, 1962, created the medal to replace the ribbon. It is awarded to any enlisted Navy reservist who fulfills certain attendance and performance requirements during a four-year period of consecutive service after July 1, 1958.

The circular medal, designed by the Institute of Heraldry, shows an old-style fouled anchor with rope. A decorative scroll around the stem reads "Meritorious Service." The design is encircled by "United States Naval Reserve" in raised letters. The reverse is blank.

The original ribbon is used; it is almost identical to that of the Naval Reserve Medal, no longer issued. A narrow center stripe of dark blue is flanked by wide stripes of dark red, thin stripes of gold, and blue stripes at the edges.

GOOD CONDUCT MEDAL

The Good Conduct Medal is neither a decoration nor a service medal. It is presented as a length-of-service award to an individual who has exhibited exemplary character, fidelity, efficiency and military deportment throughout the qualifying period.

Marine Corps

The Marine Corps Good Conduct Medal was authorized on July 20, 1896, by Special Order 49 of the Secretary of the Navy, amended many times since. It is awarded to enlisted men, either regular or Reserve, for obedience, sobriety, military efficiency, neatness, bearing, and intelligence during three years' continuous active service, if the recipient had no convictions by court martial and not more than one nonjudicial punishment.

The medal, designed by Major General Charles Heywood, U.S.M.C., ninth Commandant of the Marine Corps (1891-1903), has a gunner standing behind a naval gun of the period in the center of the obverse. This scene is encircled by a rope, with a scroll below it bearing the inscription "Semper Fidelis." The medallion is superimposed on an anchor, the stock of which appears above, slightly to the left, and the flukes below, slightly to the right. A chain joined to the anchor at the top forms a circle around the edge of the medal, with the inscription "United States Marine Corps" between it and the rope. The reverse of the medal bears the raised legend "Fidelity Zeal Obedience" about a blank area for the recipient's name. The scarlet ribbon has a navy blue center stripe. A second or subsequent award of the Good Conduct Medal is now indicated by a star.

Present type
According to new regulations, although the new medal is the same design, there is no longer a top bar suspension, and the medal is attached to the ribbon by the usual ring-and-eye. The ribbon remains the same.

Coast Guard

The Coast Guard Good Conduct Medal, authorized for issuance on December 12, 1923, is awarded to enlisted personnel of the Coast Guard and the Coast Guard Reserve for periods of service above the average. The medal was originally given for four years' consecutive service during the period from May 17, 1920, to June 30, 1934. It is now awarded for three years' consecutive service; temporary service is not applicable.

Present type

The new medal has the usual ring-and-loop top, but no longer has top and bottom slotted bars for the ribbon. The medal, reduced in size, has the seal of the Coast Guard in the center, surrounded by a circle of rope looped at the bottom. Above the circle are the words "Semper Paratus," the Coast Guard motto. Above this, near the top, is a link of naval chain, and at the bottom are crossed oars. The ribbon is maroon, with a narrow center stripe of white. Subsequent awards are indicated by stars on the ribbon.

Air Force

This medal, authorized by Congress on July 6, 1960, is awarded to enlisted men who have honorably completed three consecutive years of active service. Persons awarded this medal must have had character and efficiency ratings of excellent or higher throughout the qualifying period, including time spent in attendance at service schools, and there must have been no convictions by court martial.

During wartime the Good Conduct medal may be awarded on completion of one year of continuous service rather than three.

Designed by Joseph Kiselewski, the medal has on the obverse an eagle with wings displayed and inverted, standing on a closed book and a Roman sword. Encircling it is the inscription "Efficiency, Honor, Fidelity." The reverse has a five-pointed star, slightly above the center, with a scroll beneath for the recipient's name. Above the star are the words "For Good" and below the scroll the word "Conduct." A wreath, formed of a laurel branch on the left and an oak branch on the right, surrounds the whole design. The ribbon is light blue with three equal narrow stripes of red, white, and dark blue near the edges.

ARMED FORCES EXPEDITIONARY MEDAL

This medal was established on December 4, 1961, to be awarded to members of the United States armed forces who, after July 1, 1958, have participated in a United States military operation and encountered foreign armed opposition, or were in danger of hostile action by foreign armed forces.

The obverse has an eagle with wings raised, perched on a sword. In back of this is a compass rose, with rays coming from the angles of the compass points. This design is encircled by the inscription "Armed Forces" at the top and "Expeditionary Service" below. Between these words, completing the circle, is a sprig of laurel on each side.

The reverse has the shield as it appears on the President's seal. Below this are branches of laurel to right and left, joined in the center by a knot. At the top, in a semicircle, is the inscription "United States of America."

The ribbon has three narrow stripes of blue, white, and red in the center, flanked by wide stripes of light blue and, on each side, four equal stripes of black, brown, yellow, and green. The center stripes symbolize the United States, and the many colors at the edges symbolize other areas of the world.

The medal was awarded for service in South Vietnam, before the Vietnam Service Medal was issued.

THE VIETNAM CONFLICT

Since 1960, the United States has become increasingly more deeply involved in the Vietnam conflict. As a result, two new service medals have been created exclusively to honor the men who have served so valiantly in this struggle — one presented by the United States, and one by the government of the Republic of Vietnam.

UNITED STATES VIETNAM SERVICE MEDAL

This was created by Executive Order on July 8, 1965, signed by the President. The obverse shows a dragon behind a grove of bamboo trees. Below this design is an inscription, "Republic of Vietnam Service." The reverse shows a crossbow, the ancient weapon of Vietnam, overlaid by a burning torch, representing freedom. Around the lower edge of the medal in an arc are the words "United States of America."

The medal is awarded to all military personnel for service in Vietnam. Those who have already received the Armed Forces Medal for service in this area between July 1958 and July 3, 1965, may exchange it for this medal.

The ribbon is yellow, with three vertical red stripes in the center, suggesting the flag of the Republic of Vietnam. There is a medium green border at each edge representing the jungle.

REPUBLIC OF VIETNAM SERVICE MEDAL

This medal is authorized by the Armed Forces for wear by members of the United States Armed Forces who have served for a six-month period in Vietnam, in its surrounding waters, or in air support against an armed enemy in Vietnam any time after July 1960. The government of South Vietnam awards the ribbon, but the medal is purchased by those entitled to it. The striking design consists of a six-pointed star, enameled white, with gold edges, and a six-pointed sunburst design in gold between the arms of the star. In the center is a black enameled circle, edged in gold, and within this is the shape of Vietnam in gold; at its center are flames in red enamel.

The medal is attached to the ribbon by a design that appears on almost all the medals of Vietnam. The ribbon has a center stripe of white, flanked on either side by equal green stripes, then narrow white and green stripes at the edges. On the ribbon is attached a scroll designed in silver, with the date, "1960-   ," the blank space suitable for engraving the year that the recipient served in Vietnam.

AIR FORCE EXCEPTIONAL CIVILIAN
SERVICE AWARD

This decoration, authorized on August 30, 1948, is awarded to United States civilians, not employed by the government, who distinguish themselves by exceptional services rendered to the Department of the Air Force. It may also be awarded to any civilian, American or foreign, not employed by the government, for an act of heroism involving voluntary risk of life.

The award, designed by the United States Mint, is a circular gold-colored medal bearing the Air Force coat of arms on the obverse. It has a shield with eagle-claw baton, centered upon four crossed lightning bolts, and wings. Above this is an American eagle, wings outspread, perched on a baton. Behind the eagle is a symbolic cloud design. A laurel wreath encircles the outer edge of the medal.

The reverse is encircled by a wreath of laurel leaves tied at the bottom; within it is the inscription, "To   for exceptional civilian service to the Department of the Air Force."

The ribbon is cornflower blue, with three gold-orange dotted lines through the center.

AIR FORCE MERITORIOUS CIVILIAN
SERVICE AWARD

This decoration, authorized on August 30, 1948, was originally just a lapel pin and certificate, and evolved into its present form in 1967. The medal design is identical to that of the Exceptional Civilian Service Award of the Air Force, but it is in silver, and the inscription on the reverse is "To   for meritorious civilian service to the Department of the Air Force."

The ribbon is three equal wide bands of colors, yellow in the center, flanked on either side by light blue; within the yellow center stripe are three narrow stripes of dark blue.

AIR FORCE CIVILIAN AWARD FOR VALOR

Approved by the Secretary of the Air Force in 1965, this award is given to a civilian serving with the Air Force in any capacity who exhibits great courage, with voluntary risk of personal safety in the face of danger, beyond the call of duty, in performing an act that resulted in direct benefit to the government or its personnel. The medal, in gold, bears on the obverse the Air Force baton on an equilateral triangle surmounted by the Air Force eagle perched on a scroll inscribed with the word "Valor," all within an olive branch.

The reverse has the inscription, "Civilian award for valor, United States Air Force" circling the outer edge of the medal. "Awarded to" is inscribed above the center section, with the rest of the area blank, suitable for engraving.

The ribbon has a dark red narrow stripe in the center flanked on either side by narrow stripes of yellow, wide stripes of dark blue, narrow yellow stripes, and at the edges, wide stripes of light blue again.

AIR FORCE COMMAND CIVILIAN AWARD FOR VALOR

This medal was authorized by the same order as the above decoration and is a second-class or junior version of the first. The medal is identical to the above except that it is in silver. It is awarded for demonstrating unusual courage or competence in an emergency during performance of assigned duties. This award can be presented by the Chief of Staff, USAF, or a major commander, and, unlike the gold medal, need not be approved by the Secretary of the Air Force.

The ribbon for the medal is predominantly light blue, with four very narrow stripes of yellow near the center, and a wide stripe of red directly in the center.

MEDALS OF THE NATIONAL AERONAUTICS AND SPACE ADMINISTRATION

The National Aeronautics and Space Administration (NASA) has grown tremendously in recent years with phenomenal strides forward in space exploration. From the first man-made satellites, to the landing of our astronauts on the moon, to projected interplanetary travel, the men and women of NASA have consistently done the "impossible." And as this agency has grown, so too has its system of awards and decorations.

NASA DISTINGUISHED SERVICE MEDAL (First Design)

This decoration was established on July 29, 1959, by NASA's Civilian Space Agency. The design, by the United States Mint, is now obsolete (see next entry). A circular gold medal, it shows the official seal of NASA, a planet with a natural satellite, and another planet in the distance. In front is a wing-type satellite from lower left to upper right, and in the background are numerous stars. All this is within a circle bearing the inscription "National Aeronautics and Space Administration U.S.A." The letters and the edges of the circle are highly polished; the rest of the design is depressed and frosted. The reverse has a wreath around the edge, formed by two branches of oak leaves joined at the bottom by two acorns. Within, slightly above the center, is the inscription "Distinguished Service"; below it is a blank area suitable for engraving.

The ribbon has a thin white center stripe flanked by equally wide stripes of light, medium, dark, and navy blue.

NASA DISTINGUISHED SERVICE MEDAL

This decoration, created by NASA on July 29, 1959, and designed by the Institute of Heraldry, is the agency's highest honor. It is awarded to a person who, by distinguished service, ability and courage, has personally made a contribution representing substantial progress in aeronautical or space exploration in the interests of the United States.

The medal, in a gold finish, consists of a cross design with four large arms and four smaller ones alternately. The arms have fluted edges and are joined together by a cloud design. In the light blue enameled center is a stylized satellite streaking through an orbital circle, within a wreath of laurel, which is encompassed by a wide circle with the words "Distinguished Service N.A.S.A."

The ribbon has a wide center stripe of dark blue, flanked by narrow light blue stripes with wide medium blue stripes at the edges.

The following awards have equal rank after the Distinguished Service Medal in the NASA Incentive Awards Program.

NASA MEDAL FOR OUTSTANDING LEADERSHIP

Established by NASA on July 29, 1959, this award is given for outstanding leadership which has a pronounced effect on the aerospace technological or administrative programs of the agency. It may be given for a single accomplishment or for sustained contributions. It was designed by the Institute of Heraldry.

The medal, in gold, consists of a large circular wreath of laurel leaves, tied at the bottom. Centered in this, extending beyond the wreath, is a hand holding a torch. Behind the hand and torch is a curved tablet with the raised letters "N.A.S.A."

The ribbon has a narrow stripe of medium blue, flanked by narrow light blue stripes, and wide medium blue stripes at the edges.

NASA MEDAL FOR EXCEPTIONAL
SCIENTIFIC ACHIEVEMENT

Established by NASA on July 29, 1959, this award is given for scientific or engineering accomplishments which contribute to the programs of NASA, the Department of Defense, or other government agencies. It is given to an individual whose creative efforts are of high order and who has made important contributions to science and technology, as a scientist, an engineer, or a member of a team. It was designed by the Institute of Heraldry.

The medal, in gold, consists of a circular wreath of laurel leaves tied at the bottom, with a hand reaching up from the bottom toward a planet with an orbital halo. Behind this design is a curved tablet with the raised letters "N.A.S.A."

The ribbon has a thin center stripe of white, flanked on either side by narrow stripes of light blue, wide stripes of navy blue, narrow stripes of light blue, and wider stripes of medium blue at the edges.

NASA MEDAL FOR EXCEPTIONAL BRAVERY

Established by NASA on July 29, 1959, this award is given for exemplary and courageous handling of an emergency in NASA activities by an individual who, independent of personal danger, has acted to safeguard human life or government property; or for exemplary and courageous service by an individual in his performance, irrespective of personal danger, of an official task of importance to the mission of NASA. It was designed by the Institute of Heraldry.

The medal, in gold, consists of a circular wreath of laurel leaves tied at the bottom, with a hand reaching up from the bottom to touch a five-pointed star. Behind this design is a curved tablet with the raised letters "N.A.S.A."

The ribbon has a narrow center stripe of scarlet flanked by thin stripes of light blue, wide stripes of navy blue, thin stripes of light blue and, at the edges, stripes of medium blue.

SERVICE IN VIETNAM AWARD

Authorized by the Department of State on December 18, 1967, this medal is awarded to civilian employees of the United States Government serving in Vietnam for an aggregate of one year's service, or if the recipient's service has been discontinued because of injury or disability incurred as the result of hostile action.

The award was created because of the extraordinary and hazardous conditions of civilian service encountered in Vietnam. The department and other agencies desired to recognize the honorable performance of duty by their personnel in that country. It is comparable to the "Vietnam Service Medal" awarded to U.S. military personnel, and there is a certificate which also accompanies the presentation of the medal.

The circular medal has on the obverse a striking representation of an Oriental dragon entwined around a flaming torch of knowledge, with the word "Vietnam" at the top and "Service" at the bottom.

The reverse of the medal shows a shield within two laurel branches. The whole is enclosed by the words "Government of the United States" with two five-pointed stars.

The ribbon is dark blue with thin equal stripes of gold, red, and gold near either edge and in the center.

MERITORIOUS SERVICE MEDAL

This decoration was created by an Executive Order dated January 16, 1969. The medal was created to award to soldiers cited for outstanding non-combat achievement. It ranks between the Bronze Star and the Army Commendation medal.

The medal has on the obverse an American eagle, clutching laurel, which encompasses the bottom part of the medal, superimposed on a star with raised edges, with six decorative rays behind the star, completing the design. The medal has not yet been struck; therefore the reverse design is not known. The decoration may be awarded to any member of the United States Armed Forces.

The ribbon is of purplish-red moiré (the same as that of the Legion of Merit), with narrow white stripes near each end.

SECRETARY OF TREASURY/TRANS-
PORTATION COMMENDATION FOR
ACHIEVEMENT RIBBON

This award in the form of a ribbon only is awarded to officers and enlisted men of the United States Coast Guard and the Merchant Marine whose professional achievement exceeds normal expectancy. The ribbon bar is like that of the Navy Achievement Medal, with a narrow white stripe in the center. The ribbon is green, with two wide stripes of orange near each end and a thin white center stripe.

COMBAT ACTION RIBBON

This award was created by the Department of the Navy in February 1969. It was authorized by the Secretary of the Navy in recognition of personnel of the United States Naval Service who actively participated in ground and surface combat. It is awarded to all enlisted personnel of the Navy and the Marine Corps and to officers below the rank of captain. Those who meet the basic requirements must have been under enemy fire while actively participating in ground or surface combat. They must also have satisfactorily performed their duty while they were assigned to a unit engaged in combat or assigned to a unit for a specific combat operation.

One award of the Combat Action Ribbon is authorized to an individual for each separate war or conflict in which the requirements have been met; subsequent awards are indicated by a bronze star worn on the ribbon. The ribbon bar has three thin center stripes of red, white, and blue, to the left of center two wide stripes of blue and gold, and to the right, two wide stripes of gold and red.

VALOROUS UNIT AWARD

Army

This award, which is given after the Distinguished Unit Citation has been awarded, is conferred on units of the United States Army, and to personnel attached to cited units, for heroic combat action on or after August 3, 1963.

The degree of heroism required is the same as that which would warrant the award of a Silver Star Medal to an individual.

The Valorous Unit Award is a scarlet ribbon, with wide center stripes of red, white, and blue, as in the Silver Star Medal. This ribbon is set in a decorative metal frame simulating a laurel wreath.

MERITORIOUS UNIT COMMENDATION

Army

This award follows the above in order of rank, and it is awarded to units of the United States Army, and to personnel atached to cited units, for at least six months of outstanding service during a period of combat on or after January 1, 1944. This decoration replaces the Combat Infantryman's Badge as a unit award. The Meritorious Unit Commendation is a deep red ribbon, 1⅜ inches wide and ⅜ inch high, set in a decorative metal frame simulating a laurel wreath.

COAST GUARD UNIT COMMENDATION

Authorized by the Secretary of the Treasury, this award is presented to any ship, aircraft, or Coast Guard unit for meritorious service rendering it outstanding.

The Coast Guard Unit Commendation has a narrow white stripe in the center, flanked on either side by broad stripes of wintergreen, flanked in turn by equal stripes of red, yellow, and blue. A bronze star is worn on the ribbon for each additional commendation.

COAST GUARD RESERVE MERITORIOUS SERVICE RIBBON

This award is similar in nature to the new Naval Reserve Meritorious Service Medal. It is authorized by the Secretary of the Treasury to be awarded to enlisted personnel of the Coast Guard Reserve for four consecutive years of meritorious service in the Reserve.

The ribbon bar has a narrow stripe of white in the center, flanked by thin stripes of blue, a wide stripe of scarlet, a very thin stripe of yellow, and, at the edges, a narrow stripe of blue.

AIR RESERVE FORCES MERITORIOUS SERVICE RIBBON

This ribbon is authorized by the Secretary of the Air Force. It is awarded to personnel of the Air Reserve Forces to signify four years of continuous exemplary behavior, efficiency, and fidelity while serving in an enlisted status in the Air Reserve Forces.

The Air Reserve Forces Meritorious Service Ribbon has a very wide center stripe of light (Air Force) blue, flanked on either side by a narrow stripe of dark blue, a very thin stripe of yellow, a narrow stripe of dark blue, a narrow stripe of white, and, at the edges, a thin stripe of light blue.

APPENDIX

Chronological Table of Awards

YEAR	MEDAL	AUTHORIZATION
1780	"André Medals"	Congress
1782	Badge of Military Merit	General George Washington
1847	Certificate of Merit, Army	Congress (March 3)
1861	Medal of Honor, Navy	Congress (December 21) (Amended February 4, 1919; August 7, 1942)
1862	Medal of Honor, Army	Congress (July 12) (New design adopted December 19, 1904)
	Kearny Medal, Gold	Unofficial (November 19)
1863	Kearny Medal, Bronze	Unofficial (March 13)
	Davis Guard Medal	Unofficial (September 8)
	The Gilmore Medal	Unofficial (October 28)
1864	New Market Cross of Honor	Unofficial (May 15)
	The Army of the James Medal	Unofficial (October 11)
	Southern Cross of Honor	Unofficial
1869	Good Conduct Medal, Navy	Navy Department (April 26) (Amended November 21, 1884)
1874	Life Saving Medals	Congress (June 20) (Amended August 4, 1949)
1885	Bailey Medal	Navy Department (December 1) (Now discontinued)
1896	Good Conduct Medal, Marine Corps	Navy Department (July 20) (Amended several times, most recently July 9, 1953)
1898	Manila Bay Medal	Congress (June 3)
1900	Cardenas Medal of Honor	Congress (May 3)
1901	West Indies Naval Campaign Medal, 1898	Congress (March 3)
	Meritorious Service Medal	Congress (March 3)
1905	Certificate of Merit Medal	War Department (January 11) (Terminated by Congress July 9, 1918)
	Civil War Medal, Army	War Department (January 11)

YEAR	MEDAL	AUTHORIZATION
1905	Indian Wars Medal	War Department (January 11)
	Spanish Campaign Medal, Army	War Department (January 11)
	China Relief Expedition Medal, Army	War Department (January 11)
	Philippine Campaign Medal, Army	War Department (January 11)
1906	Philippine Congressional Medal	Congress (June 29)
1908	China Relief Expedition Medal, Navy and Marine Corps	Navy Department (June 27)
	Civil War Medal, Navy and Marine Corps	Navy Department (June 27)
	Philippine Campaign Medal, Navy and Marine Corps	Navy Department (June 27)
	Spanish Campaign Medal, Navy and Marine Corps	Navy Department (June 27)
	West Indies Campaign Medal	Navy Department (June 27)
1909	Cuban Pacification Medal, Army	War Department (May 11)
	Cuban Pacification Medal, Navy and Marine Corps	Navy Department (August 13)
1913	Nicaraguan Campaign Medal	Presidential Directive (September 22)
1915	Army of Cuba Occupation Medal	War Department (June 17)
1917	Haitian Campaign Medal, 1915	Navy Department (June 22)
	Mexican Service Medal, Army	War Department (July 6)
1918	Distinguished Service Cross, Army	Executive Order (January 2)
	Distinguished Service Medal, Army	Executive Order (January 2)
	Mexican Service Medal, Navy and Marine Corps	Navy Department (February 11)
	Mexican Border Service Medal	Congress (July 9)
	Silver Star Medal, Army	Congress (July 9) (Amended August 8, 1932)
	Spanish War Service Medal	Congress (July 9)
1919	Army of Puerto Rico Occupation Medal	War Department (February 4)

YEAR	MEDAL	AUTHORIZATION
1919	Distinguished Service Medal, Navy	Congress (February 4) (Amended August 7, 1942)
	Navy Cross	Congress (February 4) (Amended August 7, 1942)
	Victory Medal, World War I	War Department (April 9) Navy Department (July 3)
1920	Marine Corps Expeditionary Ribbon	Navy Department (March 1)
1921	Brevet Medal, Marine Corps	Navy Department (June 7)
	Dominican Campaign Medal, 1916	Navy Department (December 29)
	Haitian Campaign Medal, 1919-1920	Navy Department (December 29)
1923	Good Conduct Medal, Coast Guard	Treasury Department (December 12)
1926	Distinguished Flying Cross	Congress (July 2) (Amended by Executive Order, January 8, 1938)
	Soldier's Medal	Congress (July 2)
1929	NC-4 Medal, large gold	Congress (February 9)
	Marine Corps Expeditionary Medal	Navy Department (March 1)
	Second Nicaraguan Campaign Medal	Navy Department (November 8)
1930	Yangtze Service Medal	Navy Department (April 28)
	Byrd Antarctic Expedition Medal, 1928-1930	Congress (May 23)
1932	Purple Heart, Army	War Department (February 22)
1935	NC-4 Medal, bronze miniature	Congress (April 25)
1936	Second Byrd Antarctic Expedition Medal, 1933-1935	Congress (June 2)
	Navy Expeditionary Medal	Navy Department (August 15)
1938	Naval Reserve Medal	Navy Department (September 12) (Terminated September 12, 1958)

YEAR	MEDAL	AUTHORIZATION
1939	Organized Marine Corps Reserve Medal	Navy Department (February 19)
1940	China Service Medal	Navy Department (August 23)
1941	Army Defense Service Medal	Executive Order (June 28)
	Good Conduct Medal, Army	Executive Order (June 28) (Amended March 31, 1943; April 10, 1953)
	Army of Occupation of Germany Medal	Congress (November 21)
1942	Presidential Unit Citation, Navy	Executive Order (February 6) (Amended June 28, 1943; January 10, 1957)
	Distinguished Unit Citation, Army	Executive Order (February 26, 1942) (Superseded December 2, 1943)
	Air Medal	Executive Order (May 11) (Amended September 11)
	Legion of Merit	Congress (July 20) (Amended by Executive Order, March 15, 1955)
	Medal for Merit	Congress (July 20)
	Navy and Marine Corps Medal	Congress (August 7)
	Silver Star Medal, Navy	Congress (August 7)
	American Campaign Medal	Executive Order (November 6) (Amended March 15, 1946)
	Asiatic-Pacific Campaign Medal	Executive Order (November 6)
	European-African-Middle Eastern Campaign Medal	Executive Order (November 6) (Amended March 15, 1946)
	American Typhus Commission Medal	Executive Order (December 24)
1943	Purple Heart, Navy and Marine Corps	Navy Department (January 21) (Superseded November 12, 1952)
	Merchant Marine Distinguished Service Medal	Congress (April 11)
	Women's Army Corps Service Medal	Executive Order (July 29)
	Atlantic War Zone Bar	Congress (August 10)

YEAR	MEDAL	AUTHORIZATION
1943	Combat Bar	Congress (August 10)
	Mariner's Medal	Congress (August 10)
	Mediterranean–Middle East War Zone Bar	Congress (August 10)
	Pacific War Zone Bar	Congress (August 10)
1944	Commendation Medal, Navy	Navy Department (January 11) (Amended March 22, 1950)
	Peary Polar Expedition Medal, 1908-1909	Congress (January 28)
	Bronze Star Medal	Executive Order (February 4)
	Gallant Ship Citation Bar	Executive Order (August 29)
	Gallant Ship Medallion and Citation Plaque	Executive Order (August 29)
	Merchant Marine Defense Bar	Executive Order (August 29)
	Meritorious Service Medal, Merchant Marine	Executive Order (August 29)
	Unit Commendation, Navy	Navy Department (December 18)
1945	Selective Service Medal	Congress (July 2)
	Medal of Freedom	Executive Order (July 6) (Amended April 3, 1953)
	Victory Medal, World War II	Congress (July 6)
	United States Antarctic Expedition Medal, 1939-1941	Congress (September 24)
	Commendation Medal, Army	War Department (Medal pendant added 1949)
	Marine Corps Reserve Ribbon	Navy Department (December 17)
1946	Army of Occupation Medal	War Department (June 7)
	Merchant Marine Victory Medal	Congress (August 8)
1947	Navy Occupation Service Medal	Navy Department (January 22)
	Commendation Medal, Coast Guard	Treasury Department (August 26) (Medal pendant added July 5, 1951)
1948	Air Force Exceptional Service Award	Air Force Department (August 30)
1949	Medal for Humane Action	Congress (July 20)

YEAR	MEDAL	AUTHORIZATION
1950	American Spirit Honor Medal	Defense Department (January 27)
	Armed Forces Reserve Medal	Executive Order (September 25) (Amended March 19, 1952)
	Korean Service Medal	Executive Order (November 8)
1951	Distinguished Service Medal, Coast Guard	Treasury Department (Design approved 1962)
	Coast Guard Medal	Treasury Department (Struck 1958)
	Navy Distinguished Public Service Award	Navy Department (July 6)
	UN Service Medal	Defense Department (November 27) (Previously adopted by UN General Assembly, December 12, 1950)
1953	National Security Medal	Executive Order (January 19)
	National Defense Service Medal	Executive Order (April 22)
1954	Outstanding Unit Award, Air Force	Air Force Department (January 6)
	Exceptional Civilian Service Award	Congress
	Meritorious Civilian Service Award	Congress
1956	Korean War Service Bar	Congress (July 24)
	Distinguished Civilian Service Medal	Defense Department (September 17)
	Outstanding Civilian Service Medal	Defense Department (September 17)
1957	President's Award for Distinguished Civilian Service	Executive Order (June 27)
	Air Force Longevity Service Award Ribbon	Air Force Department (November 25)
1958	Commendation Medal, Air Force	Air Force Department (March 28)
1959	NASA Distinguished Service Medal	NASA Civilian Space Agency (July 29)

	NASA Medal for Outstanding Leadership	NASA Civilian Space Agency (July 29)
	NASA Medal for Exceptional Scientific Achievement	NASA Civilian Space Agency (July 29)
	NASA Medal for Exceptional Bravery	NASA Civilian Space Agency (July 29)
1960	Air Force Cross	Congress (July 6)
	Airman's Medal	Congress (July 6)
	Distinguished Service Medal, Air Force	Congress (July 6)
	Good Conduct Medal, Air Force	Congress (July 6)
	Medal of Honor, Air Force	Congress (July 6)
1961	Antarctica Service Medal	Congress (July 12) (Design approved 1963)
	Armed Forces Expeditionary Medal	Executive Order (December 4)
1962	Byrd Arctic Expedition Medal, 1926	Congress
	Navy Achievement Medal	Navy Department (January 24)
	Naval Reserve Meritorious Service Medal	Navy Department (June 25)
1963	Presidential Medal of Freedom	Executive Order (February 22)
	Joint Service Commendation Medal	Defense Department (June 25)
1965	Air Force Civilian Award for Valor	Air Force Department
	Air Force Combat Readiness Medal	Air Force Department
	Air Force Command Civilian Award for Valor	Air Force Department
	United States Vietnam Service Medal	Executive Order (July 8)
1967	Air Force Meritorious Civilian Service Award	
	Service in Vietnam Award	State Department (December 18)
1969	Meritorious Service Medal	Executive Order (January 16)

Bibliography

Belden, Bauman L.	*United States War Medals*. Washington: American Numismatic Society, 1915
Beyer, Walter F., and Keydel, O. F.	*Deeds of Valor* (two volumes). Detroit, Michigan: Perrien-Keydel, 1903
Blakeney, Jane	*Heroes: United States Marine Corps, 1861-1955*. Washington: Blakeney, 1957
Pershing, John J.	*My Experiences in the World War*. New York: Frederick A. Stokes, 1931
Rodenbaugh, T.F.	*Uncle Sam's Medal of Honor*. New York: Putnam, 1890
Snowden, James Ross	*Medal of Honor; Medals of Washington*. Philadelphia: Lippincott, 1862
Townsend, Edward D.	*Medals and Corps Badges of the Civil War*. New York: Appleton, 1884
United States Department of the Army	*Decorations and Awards of the Army*. Washington, 1957
United States Department of the Navy	*Navy and Marine Corps Awards Manual*. Washington, 1953
United States Printing Office	*Medal of Honor of the Navy 1861-1948*. Washington: Government Printing Office, 1949
United States Printing Office	*Medal of Honor of the United States Army*. Washington: Government Printing Office, 1948
United States War Department	*Annual Reports*. Washington, 1914-1927
Wyllie, Robert E.	*Orders, Decorations and Insignia*. New York: Putnam, 1927

"Insignia and Decorations of the U.S." *National Geographic Magazine*, October and November 1943.

Index

(Figures in italics denote pages on which descriptions of medals will be found. Dates in parentheses indicate year in which medal was authorized.)